# Managing for Stakeholders

## The Business Roundtable Institute for Corporate Ethics Series in Ethics and Leadership

The Series in Ethics and Leadership provides current and future business leaders with knowledge and insight needed to create and sustain successful organizations. The series draws on cutting-edge research from the academic world and the best thinking of business leaders, empowering practicing managers to improve the quality of their business decisions and positively affect their enterprise.

The Business Roundtable Institute for Corporate Ethics directs, manages, and edits the series. The institute is an independent entity established in partnership with Business Roundtable—an association of chief executive officers of leading corporations with a combined workforce of more than 10 million employees and $4.5 trillion in annual revenues—and leading academics from America's best business schools. The institute, housed at the University of Virginia's Darden Graduate School of Business Administration, brings together leaders from business and academia to fulfill its mission to renew and enhance the link between ethical behavior and business practice through executive education programs, practitioner-focused research, and outreach.

Information about the series and the institute can be found at www.corporate-ethics.org.

# Managing for Stakeholders

## Survival, Reputation, and Success

R. Edward Freeman

Jeffrey S. Harrison

Andrew C. Wicks

Yale University Press

New Haven & London

A Caravan book. For more information, visit www.caravanbooks.org.

Published with assistance from the Louis Stern Memorial Fund.

Designed by Nancy Ovedovitz and set in Adobe Garamond by Keystone
Typesetting, Inc. Printed in the United States of America.

Library of Congress Cataloging-in-Publication Data
Freeman, R. Edward, 1951–
Managing for stakeholders : survival, reputation, and success / R. Edward
Freeman, Jeffrey S. Harrison, Andrew C. Wicks.
p. cm. — (The Business Roundtable Institute For Corporate Ethics series in
ethics and leadership)
Includes bibliographical references and index.
ISBN 978-0-300-12528-3 (cloth : alk. paper)
1. Industrial management. 2. Corporate governance. 3. Business ethics.
4. Social responsibility of business. I. Harrison, Jeffrey S. II. Wicks,
Andrew C. III. Title.
HD31.F752 2007
658—dc22      2007013472

A catalogue record for this book is available from the British Library.

The paper in this book meets the guidelines for permanence and durability
of the Committee on Production Guidelines for Book Longevity of the
Council on Library Resources.

10  9  8  7  6  5  4  3

# Contents

# Preface

This book is the work of many people. Colleagues, co-authors, students, executives, family, and friends have all contributed to our understanding of "managing for stakeholders." In 1984 Freeman wrote *Strategic Management: A Stakeholder Approach* to try to summarize the work of authors such as Russell Ackoff, James R. Emshoff, Richard Mason, Ian Mitroff, Eric Rhenman, Eric Trist, and others—all of whom were the real pioneers of thinking about stakeholders in a business. Since 1984 many academics, executives, and other business thinkers have developed the idea that any business needs to pay attention to those groups that can affect or be affected by the business—for example, stakeholders.

*Managing for Stakeholders* is our statement of this idea more than twenty years after the publication of Freeman's book. It is written for executives, not for academics, so we have kept the references, footnotes, and other scholarly apparatus to a minimum. Many others have made points similar to the ones we make here. The current book is a summary of what we believe is the best thinking about stakeholder management, and we are grateful to the contributions of many others.

We believe that *Managing for Stakeholders* captures the essence of what it means to build and sustain a great business enterprise, large or small, in the United States and the rest of the world. We believe that it captures the essence of our system of capitalism understood as a system of social cooperation and value creation. Furthermore, we believe that it offers a roadmap to begin to put business together with ethics and values.

We desperately need a new conversation about the role of business and ethics in society. *Managing for Stakeholders* is one way into such a retelling of the story of business. We make no apologies for being capitalists at heart. We celebrate it, even though we are quite critical of the current shared understanding of capitalism as only creating value for stockholders. By the simple act of changing two letters—turning "stockholders" into "stakeholders"—we believe we can revise our understanding of capitalism to build a more robust idea of business and management.

### A NOTE ON METHOD AND DATA

Our primary concern in this book is to create a new narrative about business. Telling a new story is at once "descriptive," relating examples of where companies actually are managing for stakeholders, and at the same time "normative," suggesting how they can better manage for stakeholders. Traditional social scientific methods are inadequate as they limit themselves to describing how companies operate. New narratives are in part a description of where we are at any point in time, what our aspirations are, and what means might work so that we can fulfill our aspirations. Most academic work is in one of these areas, not all three simultaneously. There are very clear rules and methods for describing the world—the methods of empirical social science, and there are rigorous standards of logic for talking about normative or aspirational issues.

New narratives or new stories about business describe some best or new practices and go on to systematically suggest how we can enact this new story. Envisioning this new story necessarily involves pushing us beyond the stories and examples that we currently see in practice. In short, new narratives involve both our behavior and our aspirations, so it is important to ground new stories in what people are actually doing and what they could do if they adopted the new narrative. A critical part of our challenge in this book is to show how such a new story about business could be enacted in a systematic way. Although academic research has been conducted on managing for stakeholders, and while it is generally supportive of the ideas we are advancing, we have deliberately avoided a review of the academic research literature in favor of a volume that speaks to executives. We are in the process of creating a separate book that will contain all of the academic support.

We have relied on the following sources of data for the arguments in this book. First, during the past twenty-plus years we have been actively engaged in conversations with literally thousands of executives around the world. In teaching seminars, presentations, consulting engagements, and informal conversations, we have learned a great deal from them, and we have tried to represent what we have heard in these pages. Of course, we have filtered what we have heard through our own biases and hopes and dreams. We are trying to articulate what we believe is in the air, that capitalism can and should be understood as how to create value for stakeholders.

Second, we have taught thousands of MBA students who have an average of five years of real business experience. These practitioners have been demanding and have forced us to articulate what managing for stakeholders is in a way that can be effective in the short term. The data that come from these conversations have been important in trying to show how managing for stakeholders is not inconsistent with shareholder value.

Third, we are voracious readers of the business press and important secondary data sources such as newspapers, magazines, best sellers, academic articles, television, Web sites, and the like. We have tried to factor these data sources into our narrative.

We have adopted the following conventions. When a company is mentioned by name, our sources are publicly available material, except where we explicitly say, in a footnote, that the company has given us permission to use their material. When a company is referred to as ABC or XYZ, that material is from our direct experiences with particular companies who remain anonymous. We adopt a similar convention for naming particular executives, versus statements like "in the words of one CEO . . ."

We think about this book as taking these three data sources and trying to weave together a coherent story about a new way to understand business. It is driven by our interpretation of the data as well as our hopes about how to revitalize capitalism.

# Acknowledgments

The arguments in this book have been developed in a number of places over the years. We have drawn liberally from these sources, and we thank a variety of coauthors, editors, and publishers for their permission to allow us to keep the copyrights involved or to use the material in additional works.

The example of Bob Collingwood was originally developed in R. Edward Freeman, *Strategic Management: A Stakeholder Approach* (Boston: Pitman Publishing, 1984). Many of the ideas in this current book find their incubation in that earlier work. The seven techniques in Chapter 5 were largely developed at the Wharton Applied Research Center in the 1980s and have been updated here. James R. Emshoff, Arthur Finnel, Ian Mitroff (and Richard Mason), Thomas Saaty, Russell Ackoff, Eric Trist, and others around the S-cubed floor of Wharton contributed to these ideas. Unfortunately, these people cannot be held responsible as the ideas took a distinctive libertarian and capitalist turn as they encountered Freeman and Gordon Sollars. William Evan, sociologist and management theorist at Penn and Wharton, is perhaps the strongest influence on connecting these ideas with Jeffersonian ideals of ethics and freedom. These early ideas have been recast in a substantial manner here.

The ten principles of stakeholder management have been developed in R. Edward Freeman and Ramakrishna Velamuri, "A New Approach to CSR: Company Stakeholder Responsibility," in A. Kakabadse and M. Morsing (eds.), *Corporate Social Responsibility* (Hampshire, U.K.: Palgrave Macmillan, 2006), pp. 9–23.

The idea of a "names and faces" approach to managing for stakeholders was originally developed in John McVea and R. Edward Freeman, "Stakeholder Theory: A Names and Faces Approach," *Journal of Management Inquiry* 14, no. 1 (2005): 57–69.

Ideas about ethical leadership in Chapter 6 were developed in "Ethical Leadership and Creating Value for Stakeholders," in R. Peterson and O. Ferrell, *Business Ethics: New Challenges for Business Schools and Corporate Leaders* (New York: M.E. Sharpe, 2005); and in "Leading Through Values and Ethical Principles," with K. Martin, B. Parmar, P. Werhane, and M. Cording, in C. Cooper and R. Burke (eds.), *Inspiring Leaders* (Oxford, U. K.: Blackwell's, 2006).

In addition, the past twenty-five years have witnessed an explosion in the scholarship on stakeholder theory, stakeholder management, stakeholder capitalism, or as we prefer it, "managing for stakeholders." A full accounting of that scholarship, its nuances and subtleties, and especially the significant contributions of others, is one of our works in progress, tentatively titled *Stakeholder Theory: The State of the Art.* It will be a volume for academics rather than executives; however, the current book could not have been written without the theorizing, helpful criticism, and support from many people. We would especially like to mention Robert Phillips of the University of Richmond, a collaborator on many of the papers that we have written over the years, and the author of his own very fine book, *Stakeholder Theory and Organizational Ethics* (San

Francisco, Calif.: Berret Koehler, 2003), and Gordon Sollars of Fairleigh Dickenson University, our most persistent friendly critic since 1977.

We would also like to acknowledge the contributions and support of former Darden School deans John Rosenblum, Leo Hidgon, Bob Harris, and current dean Bob Bruner and the sponsor trustees of the Darden Foundation. Dean Bruner and the sponsor trustees understand, as few do, that the business world of the twenty-first century is radically different and that the Darden School, the University of Virginia, and the University of Richmond have a leading role to play in the conversation about how business and society are connected. Indeed, the very mission of the school is to inspire business leaders to create a better society. Jay Bourgeois, Richard Brownlee, Ming Jer Chin, Robert Carraway, Simone de Colle, Jacquelyn Doyle, Mark Eaker, Greg Fairchild, James Freeland, Paul Harper, Jared Harris, Mark Haskins, Alec Horniman, Lynn Isabella, Erika James, Dean Krehmeyer, Andrea Larson, Jeanne Liedtka, Marc Lipson, Luanne Lynch, Jenny Mead, Marc Modica, Brian Moriarty, Karen Musselman, David Newkirk, Bidhan Parmar, Ryan Quinn, Mark Reisler, Peter Rodriguez, James Rubin, Saras Sarasvarthy, Robert Spekman, Lisa Stewart, Elizabeth Tiesberg, Sankaran Venkataraman, Elliot Weiss, Patricia Werhane, Ron Wilcox, and other Darden, University of Virginia, and University of Richmond colleagues have all been both supportive and critical during this project.

Of special note are the classes of Darden doctoral students (too numerous to name) who have patiently pointed out the limitations of stakeholder thinking for the past dozen years or so. The members of Blues Jam are owed a special debt. For many years (since the 1960s) the Olsson family, of West Point, Virginia, has supported the idea of putting ethics together with business, and without their support of the Olsson Center for Applied Ethics this book could not have been written. In 2004 the Business Roundtable established the Business Roundtable Institute for Corporate Ethics at the Darden School, with the explicit mission to put business and ethics together to tell a new story about capitalism. The support of the CEOs of the Roundtable, in particular Franklin Raines, Steve Odland, Hank McKinnell, Chuck Prince, Anne Mulcahy, and others, has been crucial to the development of these ideas. For every Enron executive there are at least a thousand business people trying to do the right thing and create value for stakeholders. Without the full support of John Castellani, Tom Lehrer, Tita Freeman, and in its formative stages, Pat Engman and Monica Medina, the institute would not exist and we could not have written this book. The academic advisers of the institute have provided a source of academic rigor that we have kept in mind at every turn in the argument, even though we know that they do not always agree with our conclusions. In no way do we suppose that either Business Roundtable or any of the people mentioned above actually agree with our arguments here. They have been a source of inspiration, and we hope we have validated their ideas.

Outside our immediate environment we would like to thank Sybil Sachs and her colleagues and students in Zurich; Derry Harbir and his colleagues and students in Jakarta; Mette Morsing and her colleagues and students (Copenhagen Business School); Tom Jones (University of Washington); Sandra Waddock and Richard Neilsen (Boston College); Tom Donaldson and Tom Dunfee (Wharton); Joshua Margolis (Harvard Business School); Jim Walsh (Michigan); Heather Elms (American University); Shawn Berman (Santa Clara); Jamie Hendry and Michael Kramer-Johnson (Bucknell University); Terry Halbert (Temple University); Tim Fort and Jennifer Griffith (George Washington University); David Wheeler (Dalhousie University); Daniel R. Gilbert, Jr. (Gettysburg College); Ken Goodpaster, Laura Dunham, Dawn Elm, and John McVea (St. Thomas University); Mattia Gilmartin (INSEAD); Thomas Maak and Nicola Plessa (St. Gallen); Kirsten Martin (Catholic University); Ellen Auster, Andy Crane, and Dirk Matten (York University); Jeremy Moon (Nottingham University); Lorenzo Saccone (Trento University); Gianfranco Rusconi, Michele Dorigatti, and Valeria Fazio (Bergamo); Archie Carroll (University of Georgia); Juha Nasi (Jyvas-kyla University); Jim Post (Boston University); Lee Preston (University of Maryland); Norm Bowie (University of Minnesota); Ron Meeks (Mercer Delta); and countless others who have helped us think about these issues over the years. We are especially grateful to Mike O'Malley, Jessie Hunnicutt, Joyce Ippolito, Dan Heaton, Alex Larson, and the entire Yale University Press team.

# Managing for Stakeholders

# 1

## Managing for Stakeholders

Bob Collingwood was president of Woodland International, a division of a large company headquartered in the United States with operations in fifty-five countries around the world. His twenty-year business career had been marked by significant changes at Woodland and in the business environment in which Woodland had grown and operated. Bob's responsibilities included overseeing manufacturing as well as public affairs, and he had bottom-line responsibility for the fully integrated Woodland operations. He was measured on "economic value added" as well as several other variables.[1] As Bob checked his calendar for the upcoming two weeks, he could see that his schedule was even more hectic than usual. He had appointments with government officials at the national level to discuss some legislation that affected Woodland. He had to fly to Mississippi to discuss a potential new plant with state officials. He had a meeting with several environmentalists to discuss a joint venture on waste reduction that was a new partnership between industry and these activists. He had a day-long meeting scheduled to brainstorm how the company could take more advantage of its Web site and of the Internet in general. The new labor contract was up for renewal, and rumors of restructurings and layoffs were plentiful. In addition, he had important meetings with his counterparts at three customer accounts. In four days he had to be in Tokyo for twenty-four hours to launch a new office and a new marketing effort, only to jet back to Texas for a two-day strategy meeting.

Each day Bob had several hundred e-mail messages, most of which his staff could handle, and his voice mailbox was constantly full. He received an average of forty-five faxes a day. He had a committed team of people, most of whom he had been personally able to select, and each of whom experienced roughly the same level of work and resulting stress as he did.

As Bob thought about the enormous amount of effort that went on to prepare himself and Woodland for the upcoming two weeks he couldn't help but wonder how things could be more hectic. Collingwood had risen rapidly at Woodland International and was headed for "stardom" in company headquarters, mentioned frequently as a candidate for future CEO. He did not feel prepared to handle the diverse mix of situations he now faced, and furthermore, he had a sinking feeling that the air of crisis that seemed to hang over him and his staff would never go away. He had missed his children's last two Little League games and a piano recital, and he increasingly felt that both his professional and personal lives were spinning out of control.[2]

Although Bob and his people had the skills and abilities to meet each situation and to manage the crises as they came up on a daily basis, they were unable to preempt the situations. Bob knew that he needed a framework, a mindset, and some different methods and processes for leading the organization forward. He needed to somehow redefine the idea of constantly being behind the eight ball each and every day. He knew that he had to escape the crisis-reaction-crisis cycle or risk burning out both his people and himself.

This book is about Bob and the thousands of managers around the world like him who meet all the criteria for good managers and leaders, yet who do not seem to be able to get ahead of the curve in today's fast-changing business environment. It explains a framework for business and management, "managing for stakeholders," which offers a mindset for Bob and his colleagues to begin to interpret their world differently and to lead in a more positive fashion.

### MANAGING FOR STAKEHOLDERS: THE BASIC IDEA

We need a new way to think about business. Executives in the past twenty-five years have witnessed unprecedented changes, and the dominant models and frameworks that we use to understand business cannot easily account for these changes. From the globalization of capital markets to the emergence of powerful information technologies, the very nature of the modern corporation has changed virtually beyond recognition.

The purpose of this book is to set forth a new conceptualization of business and the role of the executive. This new view, which we call managing for stakeholders, has emerged during the past twenty-five years from the work of many business thinkers and the actions of executives around the world.[3]

The basic idea is quite simple. Business can be understood as a set of relationships among groups that have a stake in the activities that make up the business. Business is about how customers, suppliers, employees, financiers (stockholders, bondholders, banks, and so on), communities, and managers interact and create value. To understand a business is to know how these relationships work. The executive's or entrepreneur's job is to manage and shape these relationships, hence the term "managing for stakeholders."

Customers, suppliers, employees, financiers, communities, and managers are all key parts of today's business organization. If we understand capitalism as how business really works (rather than how theorists want us to believe it works) it will become obvious that this has always been true. Building and leading a great company has always been about managing for stakeholders. The idea that we need to pay attention to only one of these groups, the people that supply the capital (stockholders or financiers), if we want to build and sustain a successful business is deeply flawed. The very nature of capitalism itself is putting together a deal, a contract, or a set of relationships among stakeholders so that all can win continuously over a long period of time.

## BUSINESS REALITY

There is a very pragmatic reason to adopt a "managing for stakeholders" view: it is what any successful business really does. Managers have to concentrate on creating and sustaining value for key stakeholders, no matter what the overall purpose or direction of a particular business is. So, even if the ideologues who insist that the only legitimate purpose of a business is to maximize shareholder value or maximize profits, the only way to do that is to create great products and services that customers want to buy. Even in these narrowly defined businesses, managers must pay attention to supplier and employee relationships, and if they are at all clever they will understand that paying attention to community can help prevent activists, regulators, and others from using the political process to prevent their companies from pursuing profits. And, of course, executives do have to pay attention to pursuing profits for stockholders or financiers and creating value for other stakeholders at the same time. Business, indeed any business, just is creating value for stakeholders. The day-to-day life of any business consists of interactions with a broad range of stakeholders, and these relationships need to be managed in a thoughtful way.

In summary, even if the executives and directors of a firm believe that creating shareholder value is the only legitimate objective for business, they must concentrate on *stakeholder* relationships to accomplish the creation of shareholder value. The logic is simple. The business world today is very complex and there is a great deal of uncertainty. It consists of interconnected networks of customers, suppliers, communities, employees, and financiers that are vital to the achievement of business success. The company that manages for shareholders at the expense of other stakeholders cannot sustain its performance. A system of economic activity based on such exclusive attention to shareholders is rife for social activism and regulation in a free society on behalf of the other stakeholders.

## WHAT BUSINESS CAN BE

Many critics of the idea of managing for stakeholders suggest that it encourages business leaders to focus their attention on non-business activities. Nothing could be further from the truth. There is really no inherent conflict between the interests of financiers and other stakeholders. If we are correct, there is simply no way to maximize value for financiers without paying attention to the other stakeholders. But, there is more.

The past century and surely the next one will yield unprecedented economic and technological progress. That progress is largely due to the ability of entrepreneurs and other business leaders to create value for their stakeholders. Thinking about business more broadly, in stakeholder terms, is an idea that potentially frees capitalism from its position as a social institution that is morally and ethically suspect simply because "it's all about the money." Of course, the money is important, but so is the value created for customers, employees, suppliers, and communities.

Some businesses really do try to maximize value for financiers, but most do not. Most have a different sense of purpose or what they stand for that usually includes creating value for at least customers and employees. Some businesses even have a more "noble cause" approach and are trying to change society. Most want to create value that allows people to improve their lives and to flourish. Managing for stakeholders is a multifaceted idea that allows us to see that there are many ways to successfully manage a business. If business as an institution is to be healthy, thrive, and make our lives better, this diversity of management methods and ideas is good in itself.

### CAPITALISM AND THE LOGIC OF VALUES

Business works because of the "logic of values," the way that values form the very foundation of economic activity. In the business world of the twenty-first century the very purpose of a business in society is connected with creating value for stakeholders. We can better understand business by seeing it as an institution for stakeholder interaction. Corporations are just the vehicles by which stakeholders are engaged in a joint and cooperative enterprise of creating value for each other. Capitalism, in this view, is primarily a cooperative system of innovation, value creation, and exchange. Indeed it is the most powerful method of social cooperation we have ever invented. Competition is a second-order, emergent property that adds fuel to the fire of innovation. Business works, in this "stakeholder capitalism" view, because people want to innovate and create together, not simply because they are competitive.

### MANAGING FOR STAKEHOLDERS: THE BASIC PICTURE

Figure 1.1 depicts this basic idea for adopting a "managing for stakeholders" view.[4] First of all, we have defined a stakeholder as any group or individual who can affect or is affected by the achievement of a corporation's purpose. Those groups in the inner circle, which we will call primary stakeholders, define most businesses. Clearly, managers need to pay a special kind of attention to these groups. They need

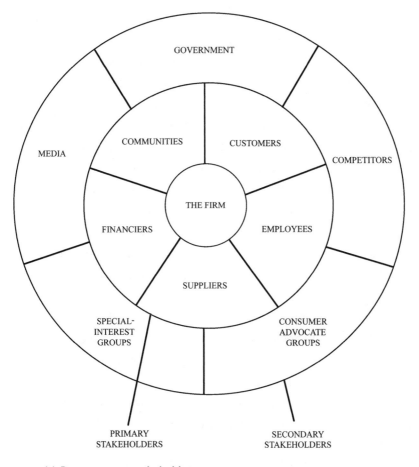

1.1. Basic two-tier stakeholder map

to understand the values and purposes that are at stake among customers, suppliers, financiers, communities, and employees. The interests of these groups go a long way in explaining whether or not a company is built to last, whether it can achieve and sustain extraordinary performance. It would be difficult to understand a framework that did not take into account relationships among customers, suppliers, employees, and financiers, as our main model of business and management is built on better serving these groups. At least in a relatively free and open society, however, community must also be on that short list of primary stakeholders. The litany of community members using the political process to regulate the firm is long and dreary, and it exists largely because our framework of business has ignored community as an important stakeholder.

The outer ring of the diagram in Figure 1.1 shows another set of groups that can affect or be affected by the corporation. Each of these can influence the relationship of the corporation with the primary stakeholders. Environmentalists can influence how a corporation deals with community or with a segment of customers. Government can drastically alter the design and delivery of products and services, and it affects each of the primary stakeholder relationships since it regulates the flow of information to financiers as well as the set of permissible practices with employees.

Figure 1.1 represents those thinkers and managers who believe that we should define stakeholders in very narrow terms, by including only those groups who have high legitimacy (primary stakeholders). It takes into account those strategists who have argued that if a group can affect the corporation, even indirectly, then the company needs to think strategically about its relationship with that group.[5]

A specific company's stakeholder map may differ from Figure 1.1. Companies in the defense industry have governments as primary stakeholders. Companies in the toxic waste disposal business may need to consider environmentalists as primary stakeholders. Who is a primary stakeholder and who is an instrumental stakeholder depends in large part on the company's overall purpose.

Our argument is simple. The stakeholder framework depicted in Figure 1.1 and sketched in the remainder of this book must underlie any practical theory or model about business—at least in today's world filled with change. There are many ways to define and depict the stakeholders in a business, and we shall return to this point in Chapter 3.

## THE ROLE OF CHANGE

There are at least four major trends, each of which has had profound effects on business. First, few people are arguing that we need more government planning and control of private business. Indeed, around the world, governments have been exiting markets, leaving business to private parties, and selling their stakes in industry after industry through privatization, while often retaining intense regulatory control. Markets have become much more open and liberal, and while there is still steady pressure for regulation, most policy makers around the globe realize that basic processes of markets, companies, and investments are the keys to prosperity.

Second, along with the liberalization of markets has come a liberalization of political institutions around the world. The fall of communism, the pressure for more market-oriented reform in countries as different as Japan and Indonesia, the market reforms in China, the openings of once closed societies have all had a tremendous impact on the opportunities available for businesses. Business today is global in unprecedented ways.

Third, over the past few decades we have discovered that we need to take better care of our environment. This environmental awareness, led by nongovernmental organizations (NGOs), has spread around the world, and it has led to a wealth of innovation in business. 3M sells products from its waste stream. Companies like Patagonia make useful products out of what once would have been garbage. Even the U.S. automobile manufacturers are inventing new technologies that make the internal combustion engine cleaner. In addition, many have argued that environmental values are only the start. Businesses can and should pay attention to other societal issues like public health, education, and other issues where the effects of business matter to broader "civil society." One trend that has exploded is the whole field of social investing.

More than $2 trillion has been invested specifically in companies that meet criteria relating to their effects on society.[6]

Finally, these three trends are fueled by a fourth one: the impressive advances in information technology. The information revolution has made it possible for businesses around the globe to see vast improvements in productivity and innovation. Today's world is connected, plugged in, turned on, and wireless. Information technology has changed the very nature of the way that we work with each other, emphasizing knowledge over place.

Each of these trends has added a layer of complexity and intensity to stakeholder relationships. Whether, as IBM says, it is an "on demand" world, or whether the interconnections among stakeholders make communication much easier, there are few secrets in today's world. Executives live in the fishbowl, on full display. They need a way of thinking that easily integrates the many changes that they face. Focusing simply on stockholders and shareholder value is not helpful.

### ADOPTING THE STAKEHOLDER MINDSET

Adopting the stakeholder mindset means understanding that business just is creating value for stakeholders. From startups to large bureaucratic firms, business works when customers, suppliers, employees, communities, and financiers get their needs and desires satisfied over time. The key insight of managing for stakeholders is that the interests of these groups must go together over time. A business that constantly trades off the interests of one group for another is doomed for trouble and failure.

Seeing stakeholder interests as joint rather than opposed is difficult. It is not always easy to find a way to accommodate all stakeholder interests. It is easier to trade off one versus another. Why not delay spending on new products for customers in order to keep earnings a bit higher? Why not cut employee medical benefits in order to invest in a new inventory control system?

The stakeholder mindset asks executives to reframe the questions. How can we invest in new products and create higher earnings? How can we be sure our employees are healthy and happy and are able to work creatively so that we can capture the benefits of new information technology such as inventory control systems? Our current way of thinking about business and management simply asks the wrong question. It asks how we should distribute the burdens and benefits among stakeholders. The managing for stakeholders mindset asks how we can create as much value as possible for all of our stakeholders. In a recent book reflecting on his experience as CEO of Medtronic, Bill George summarized the managing for stakeholders mindset: "Serving all your stakeholders is the best way to produce long term results and create a growing, prosperous company. . . . Let me be very clear about this: there is no conflict between serving all your stakeholders and providing excellent returns for shareholders. In the long term it is impossible to have one without the other. However, serving all these stakeholder groups requires discipline, vision, and committed leadership."[7]

### ENTERPRISE STRATEGY AND THE CONNECTION TO ETHICS AND VALUES

Once you begin to think about business as creating value for stakeholders, it is easy and necessary to take the next step: to begin to see the process of value creation as inherently concerned with ethics and values. Ethics and values questions are at the core of *Managing for Stakeholders,* since executives early on in the process must address just who are the stakeholders for whom they are creating value.

Part of the problem in today's highly charged business environment with clarion calls for more attention to ethics rests on an understanding of business where ethics is separated from business. And, there is some truth in these calls for reform. We do need more ethics in business. But, an even better idea would be to change the way we think about business so that we could be sure that ethics gets built into the very foundations of business. The aim of managing for stakeholders is to make such a change and to suggest a more appropriate view of capitalism.

The beauty of capitalism is that there are multiple ways to create value for stakeholders. Also, there are many choices of which stakeholders to serve. Only by being very clear about values, individual and corporate, can executives begin to harness the power of managing for stakeholders.

Managing for stakeholders relies on a concept called enterprise strategy that replaces the standard questions of corporate strategy such as "what business are we in" with questions that come logically prior. Managing in an ever-changing world filled with conflict and stakeholders means that we have to answer questions like "How do we make each of our stakeholders better off?" "What do we stand for?" "Which stakeholders do we want to serve?" "What are our aspirations?" and "What legacy or impact do we want to leave on the world?" These questions imply that we cannot ignore basic ethics and values in business. We can no longer pretend to separate out the business from the ethics. We cannot afford another wave of scandals like Enron, Arthur Andersen, Tyco, and the like. One way to avoid this kind of thing is to replace the shareholders-only model with something like the managing for stakeholders concept.

Enterprise-level strategy is a four-part idea.[8] To begin, a business must have a clear purpose: something that resonates enough with key stakeholders to get them to "come to the party" and trade with the business. For established companies like Wal-Mart or Merck these purposes have been clearly articulated in the slogans "everyday low price" or "inventing medicine to save lives." Jim Collins and Jerry Poras have documented the existence of purpose in companies that have been "built to last." For other companies who do not have such a history, perhaps their purpose has not been so clearly articulated, so there is much work to be done. Purpose is the reason for showing up. Even the smallest startup must give customers and employees reasons for showing up and engaging in value creation and trade. A business can't get off the ground without an initial commitment of customers and other stakeholders.

Next, there has to be a reason for having an ongoing relationship with the business, so there must be a set of principles or policies that garner and build stakeholder commitment over time. For instance, at Wal-Mart customers have to come to realize that everything that Wal-Mart does is aimed at creating "everyday low price"; there is a predictability and consistency to that relationship.

Third, enterprise strategy must recognize that societal expectations play a role in the process of creating and sustaining value for stakeholders. When a company is going against the grain of society, it must realize that it is doing so and put in place a strategy that tries to mitigate the societal effects of its actions. For instance, Wal-Mart has been criticized for ruining Main Street and replacing Mom and Pop shops. In several localities in the United States, specific anti–Wal-Mart zoning rules have been enacted. Wal-Mart's response seems to be that Wal-Mart customers vote with their dollars every day and that Mom and Pop shops are going out of business because Wal-Mart offers a better value. Despite the fact that the company may have "right" on its side, Wal-Mart executives still need to understand exactly where they might be going against the society's grain. They must put in place some ideas that might ameliorate these effects if possible.

Finally, enterprise strategy must be executed in the spirit of ethical leadership. Given that there are multiple stakeholders, a complex business environment, and an increasingly demanding public that expects the worst from business, we must build ethics into the foundations of how value gets created. Leaders can't claim they did not know something wrong was being done. They can't pretend that they do not live in a fishbowl. And, more importantly, most business people are in fact

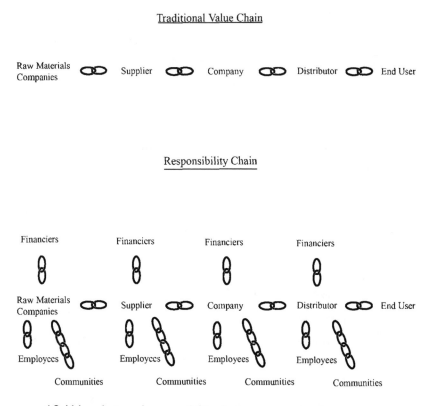

1.2. Value chain and responsibility chain

good, ethical people. We need a framework that expects them to be ethical leaders rather than to stick with the current view of capitalists as a bunch of "greedy little bastards" trying to do each other in.

Enterprise strategy is about managing the total enterprise. It is about the complete chain of value creation and trade from raw materials to end use. Traditionally we could think of a firm as responsible for only a part of the value creation chain. Society held firms accountable for how they modified what suppliers sold them. The responsibility was seen as discrete and limited. If a company made a faulty product it was of course responsible, but it was limited to its own actions. Increasingly today the chain of value has become a chain of responsibility. As Figure 1.2 shows, companies are being held accountable for the effects of their actions, the effects of their stakeholders' actions throughout the value chain. Nike is held accountable for the labor practices of its suppliers. Food and beverage companies are increasingly being held accountable for the effects of their products. Without a clear sense of what you stand for, it is just impossible to work through this thicket of stakeholders and issues.[9]

## EVERYDAY BUSINESS PROCESSES

The stakeholder mindset and the idea of enterprise strategy must ultimately permeate all the way through the business. Over the past twenty years a number of techniques have been developed to assist executives in managing key stakeholder relationships. For starters, we need to take a fairly detailed approach to define who our stakeholders are. Segmentation analysis can be applied across stakeholder groups, not just according to customers or markets. Stakeholder thinking must also be based on realistic assessments of stakes and behavior. In a world of politics and political spin, where every nuance of a strategy can be analyzed publicly, we need to think about concrete stakeholder behavior.

Creating value for stakeholders is about understanding and satisfying their needs and concerns. Executives need to understand in detail each stakeholder's: (1) actual or current behavior; (2) its cooperative potential, or how it could help a firm achieve its purpose; and (3) its competitive threat, how it could prevent a firm from achieving its purpose. Managing stakeholder relationships effectively is less about stakeholders' attitudes and more about their behavior and their beliefs about the business. If a particular stakeholder group thinks that a firm simply doesn't want to meet their needs, or puts the needs of other groups ahead of theirs, there will likely be little commitment and the group's behavior is likely to pose a competitive threat, ultimately leaving the value-creation process.

In addition to approaching managing for stakeholders on a stakeholder-by-stakeholder basis, executives also have to integrate across stakeholder groups. The key is finding strategies and programs that appeal to and satisfy multiple stakeholder groups simultaneously. For instance, it is one thing to satisfy an environmental group by building cars that get better gas mileage, but quite another to satisfy other important market segments like government regulators and shareholders by building an SUV that gets great gas mileage and is profitable.

There are four possible approaches for designing bottom-line processes for dealing with stakeholders. Obviously, a company can simply ignore a stakeholder, do nothing, and allocate no resources. In some instances this is a viable approach. Often it isn't done intentionally, but a particular stakeholder group just falls through the cracks. A second strategy is what we'll call the "public relations approach," in which executives decide on the company story and use strategies like image advertising, communicating with opinion leaders, and so on to get the story known. Again, this is sometimes warranted and effective, but in today's business world there can also be a high degree of skepticism among some constituencies, depending on a company's track record. Third, the company can engage in implicit negotiation. In this view, executives take stakeholders' positions into account in formulating strategy but have little direct interaction and negotiation with them. Obviously, this strategy is only as good as the information about a particular stakeholder's needs and wants.

In more and more cases, executives need an overall strategic posture of direct contact and direct negotiation and communication with stakeholders. Over the years this has come to be called stakeholder engagement. It is often the easiest way to find win-win solutions, and communicating in good faith builds relationships. Such explicit negotiation and communication can no longer be planned. It often takes time, with a great deal of give and take. The results are a fluidity in stakeholder relationships and an ambiguity that can be difficult to manage. The process calls for a different idea of leadership.

## THE ROLE OF LEADERSHIP

No single topic takes up more space on business bookshelves than that of leadership. The truth is, we don't know very much about leadership despite all of the studies and examples from history that we have. Some have even questioned the usefulness of "leadership" as a concept.

In a practical sense, chief executive officers (CEOs) talk a lot about "tone at the top," by which they mean top management setting the example for the behavior of others or providing a role model that hopefully cascades down the organization. The idea of "tone at the top" connects leadership and ethics. It is there that we find some of the biggest abuses of the recent scandals. From throwing lavish, multimillion-dollar birthday parties to publicly applauding someone for "stealing" the resources to start a business, executive leadership behavior makes a real difference. This is especially true in a world where there are multiple stakeholder pressures, conflicting values, and a standard mindset that in the end, executives only have to worry about shareholders. Therefore we must search for a set of connections between ethics and leadership that enables executives to set the right tone at the top that will promote the creation of value for all of the stakeholders.

We suggest that there are three types of leaders: (1) the amoral leader; (2) the values-based leader; and (3) the ethical leader.

The notion of the *amoral leader* focuses on the aspects of leadership that emphasize getting things done. Perhaps amoral leaders eventually evaluate the outcomes that result from such leadership and judge them to be good or bad, but that is a job for Monday morning quarterbacks. This way of connecting, or not connecting, ethics and leadership focuses on getting results. In our experience in business, almost no one starts out to be an amoral leader, but many executives end up as one because they do not keep values and ethics questions front and center.

The *values-based leader* and those thinkers who recommend such an approach recognize that values are an important part of the tasks of leadership. They believe that a true leader must be of good character and stand for such values as honesty, respect, and integrity. They focus on a character- or virtue-based view of ethics, relying on the authenticity and drive of the leader to do the right thing. While there is nothing wrong with such an approach, it is not sufficient in today's world. There are too many conflicts, too many "right answers," and too many stakeholder relationships to be balanced. Values are important, and good leaders have to know their own values and the values of other stakeholders, but they have to do more.

The *ethical leader* is committed to a process of examining values, principles, harms and benefits, issues of character, the effectiveness of stakeholder relationships, and other complex issues in a multicultural setting. Issues of culture, power, gender, race, sexuality, age, and ability are all complex and center stage, and the ethical leader must deal with these issues. The tasks of the ethical leader require both curiosity and humility in addition to the fierce determination to accomplish results. Ethical leaders must be able to articulate and embody how their business makes each key stakeholder better off, or what the business is doing to improve the tradeoffs among stakeholders. Ethical leaders must have a clear definition of what they stand for, and they must be engaged in the societal conversations about how business can make society better. We'll have more to say about the tasks of the ethical leader in Chapter 6, but suffice it to say now that managing for stakeholders requires that ethics and leadership go together.

We shall proceed along the following lines. Chapter 2 explores the changes in business that have made managing for stakeholders necessary. Chapter 3 describes the basic mindset and framework of managing for stakeholders. It describes a set of principles that underlie our approach and shows how these principles have to be applied at three levels: the business as a whole; the business processes that are used to manage stakeholders; and the day-to-day transactions with key stakeholders.

In Chapter 4 we detail the idea of "enterprise strategy" and show that it combines the best in strategic thinking with the best in ethical thinking. It goes hand in hand with a company's vision and values. We suggest how a managing for stakeholders approach can be used to connect business with values and ethics and with corporate social responsibility. We give many examples of companies that have made these ideas work.

In Chapter 5 we build on our many years of watching businesses manage stakeholder relationships and our experience in helping some of these companies do it better. We suggest seven concrete and practical techniques for creating value for stakeholders. All of these techniques are aimed at the real world of practical, day-to-day interactions with stakeholders.

In Chapter 6 we return to the big picture and show how managing for stakeholders requires a new kind of business leader: one that we call the ethical leader. We make some suggestions about how executives can work to become ethical leaders and we look at some common pitfalls.

Finally, in the Appendix we address some of the frequently asked questions about managing for stakeholders and, indirectly, some of the myths and false ideas that have grown up around the stakeholder concept in the past twenty-five years.

We hope to at least give one perspective that sets managing for stakeholders on a course that is decidedly pro-business and one that both celebrates the triumphs and achievements of our system of value creation and trade, and acknowledges the difficulties and challenges in today's business environment.

# 2

## Business in the Twenty-first Century

As Bob Collingwood reclined his seat in the corporate jet, he thought about the upcoming two weeks. While he knew he could survive them, he was not sure how long he could avoid burnout. He had seen it happen to many of his peers. They got to a certain point and either professionally self-destructed by making a series of risky and unwise decisions, or their personal lives collapsed into a set of broken promises and commitments. Bob was determined to avoid both paths.

He recalled his two years at a top MBA program some fifteen years before. He had learned a lot of new skills, especially how to analyze a business into its simplest parts, and put it back together again. These were not just financial and quantitative skills. He had paid attention when his professors in the "human" courses told him that all he had to accomplish something were the people who worked for him. It just wasn't enough. Of course he needed better market analysis, better finance numbers, and better human resources. But the pace of change seemed to defy just working harder with the tools he had, even though he had tried to stay up to date. Bob needed something else—something to help him think through the real world of business, a world defined by tremendous change and turbulence.

### THE PROBLEM OF CHANGE

Business has changed in some pretty basic ways. Our theories and models have not kept pace with these changes. Consequently, the air of crisis, inadequacy, and rapid change that affects most businesses today is not likely to settle down. Books on business top the best-seller list, each offering a magical piecemeal cure. What we need is a new way to think about the fundamentals of business and management.

The purpose of this chapter is to lay out some of the changes that have affected our understanding of business, and to suggest that we need a framework of "managing for stakeholders" in order to continue the incredible value creation engine that is capitalism. Before saying more about managing for stakeholders it is important to clarify the need for such a new framework. In fact the changes that Bob Collingwood and others like him have witnessed are unprecedented in the history of business. These changes make our current way of understanding both business and capitalism woefully inadequate.

### THE DOMINANT FRAMEWORK: MANAGERIAL CAPITALISM

The modern business corporation emerged during the twentieth century as one of the most important innovations in human history. Yet the changes that we are now experiencing call for its reinvention. Before we suggest what this revision, which we call "managing for stakeholders" or "stakeholder capitalism," is, first we need to understand how the dominant story came to be told.

Somewhere in the past, organizations were quite simple, and "doing business" consisted of buying raw materials from suppliers, converting it to products, and selling it to customers. For the most part owner-entrepreneurs founded such simple businesses and worked at the business along with members of their families. The family-dominated business still accounts for a large proportion of the new business starts today, and this is true around the globe. The development of new production processes, such as the assembly line, meant that jobs could be specialized and more work could be accomplished. New technologies and sources of power became readily available. Demographic factors began to favor the concentration of production in urban areas. These and other social and political forces combined to require larger amounts of capital, well beyond the scope of most individual owner-manager-employees. Additionally, workers or non-family members began to dominate the firm and were the rule rather than the exception.

Ownership of the business became more dispersed as capital was raised from banks, stockholders, and other institutions. Indeed, the management of the firm became separated from the ownership of the firm. And, in order to be successful, the top managers of the business had to simultaneously satisfy the owners, the employees and their unions, suppliers, and customers. This organizational system of business was known as managerial capitalism or laissez faire capitalism, and more recently as shareholder capitalism. We will often call it the "managerial view" to distinguish it from the "stakeholder view" or "managing for stakeholders."[1]

As businesses grew and as operations became dispersed, managers developed a means of control via the divisionalized firm. Led by Alfred Sloan at General Motors, the divisionalized firm with a central headquarters staff was widely adapted.[2] The dominant model for managerial authority was the military and civil service bureaucracy. The creation of rational structures and processes allowed the orderly progress of business growth to be well managed.

Managerialism, hierarchy, stability, and predictability all evolved together, in the United States and Europe, to form the most powerful economic system in the history of humanity. The rise of bureaucracy and managerialism was so strong that the economist Joseph Schumpeter predicted that it would wipe out the creative force of capitalism, stifling innovation in its drive for predictability and stability.[3]

During the past thirty years this managerial model has put shareholders at the center of the firm as the most important group for managers to worry about. This mindset has dealt with the increasing complexity of the business world by focusing more intensely on shareholders and creating value for shareholders. It has become common wisdom to increase shareholder value, and many companies have instituted complex incentive compensation plans aimed at aligning the interests of executives with the interests of shareholders. These incentive plans are often tied to the price of a company's stock, which is affected by many factors, not the least of which is the expectations of Wall Street analysts about earnings per share each quarter. Meeting Wall Street targets and forming a stable and predictable base of quarter over quarter increases in earnings per share has become the standard for measuring company performance. Indeed, all of the recent scandals at Enron, WorldCom, Tyco, Arthur Andersen, and others are in part due to relying on increasing shareholder value, sometimes in opposition to accounting rules and law. Unfortunately, the world has changed so that the stability and predictability required by the shareholder approach can no longer be assured.

## CHANGE AND THE MANAGERIAL VIEW OF BUSINESS

The managerial view of business with shareholders at the center is inherently resistant to change. It puts shareholders' interests over and above the interests of customers, suppliers, employees, and others, as if these interests must conflict with each other. It understands a business as an essentially hierarchical organization fastened together with

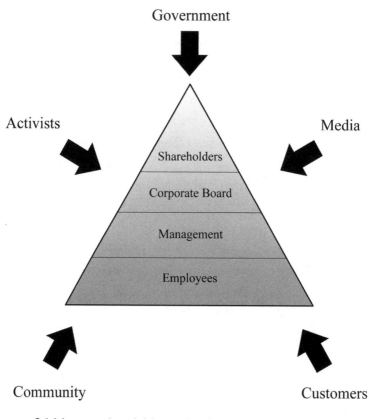

Government

Activists

Media

Shareholders

Corporate Board

Management

Employees

Community

Customers

2.1. Managerial model: hierarchical view

authority to act in the shareholders' interests. Figure 2.1 depicts this hierarchical model. Executives often speak in the language of hierarchy, saying "we work for the shareholders," "shareholders are the boss," and "you have to do what the shareholders want." According to this interpretation, change should occur only when the shareholders are unhappy, and as long as executives can produce a series of incrementally better results there is no problem. In fact there have been numerous cases of companies missing earnings expectations by as little as a penny, and the stock getting hammered.

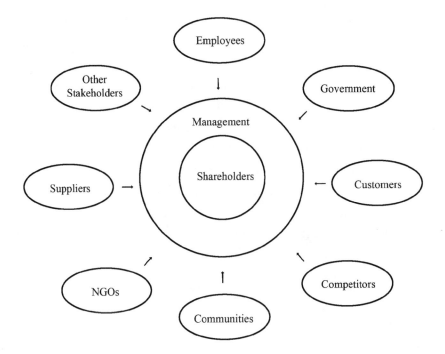

2.2. Managerial model: inward-focus view

Figure 2.2 shows how the managerial view is inwardly focused. By paying so much attention to the interests of one stakeholder group—shareholders—managers fail to look externally for new sources of growth and innovation. The interests of customers and employees are often traded off (falsely, usually) with the interests of shareholders. Under conditions of uncertainty these tradeoffs usually have unpredictable consequences that turn out to be negative.

## CHANGE IN THE BUSINESS WORLD OF THE TWENTY-FIRST CENTURY

The business world of today has undergone real change from a number of directions, and predictability and stability are increasingly nowhere to be found. Change has occurred along three dimensions of business, and each has had a profound effect on executives like Bob Collingwood.

First, there are at least four macro changes that make business more complex and uncertain. Second, the critical relationships that define a business—those with customers, suppliers, employees, communities, and owners—have experienced substantial change as we begin the twenty-first century. Finally, the ability of other groups and individuals to influence these primary relationships has changed dramatically, making governments, environmentalists, interest groups, the media, and even illegal groups relevant to business.

## FOUR MACRO CHANGES IN BUSINESS

### The Liberalization of Markets

During the rise of the dominant framework of managerial capitalism the world was engaged in an ideological war; free markets versus state-owned and state-planned industry. For many complicated reasons this war is over, and free markets have been declared the winner. And how free markets have won! Trade barriers are falling. Governments are privatizing their state-owned businesses. Everyone is getting into the act. The last bastions of monopoly, the utilities, are preparing for competition, and in some places like Great Britain and New Zealand, such competition is already a fact of life.

The result is that business is global today in ways that were unimaginable a few short years ago. Markets for everything from capital to blue jeans are understandable on a global level. If Bob Collingwood is to be effective he must find a business strategy that makes sense in Jakarta and in Omaha, and he must build an organization that can work effectively in a multitude of settings. When markets become more global, people and organizations have to follow.

## The Liberalization of Political Institutions

At the same time that markets have opened up and become more global in nature, political institutions have become more liberalized and more open. From the scandals that have enveloped Washington and Tokyo to the fall of the Berlin Wall, politicians must live in the fishbowl of modern technological life. The results have been astounding. Who could have predicted the fall of communism in the former Soviet Union and the Eastern Bloc? Even China has gone a long way to adopt market reforms in the midst of a regime that is still communist in name. There is pressure for more democratic reform in the Asian tiger countries as well, as the economies have faltered recently due in large part to the loss of confidence by investors in the kind of closed-loop crony capitalism that still exists in places such as Indonesia. The rise of the women's movement, the emergence of the political questions of minorities' rights, and the global human rights movement in general has meant that people put less and less trust in their governments, creating pressure for more democratic reform. This democratic reform has been sponsored in part by the new information technology. It is a wonderful irony that the old Soviet news service, Tass, has been leapfrogged by a news service called Interfax.

The impact on business is enormous. The past ten years have seen the emergence of new (and sometimes unsavory) forms of capitalism in former socialist countries. Motorola, AT&T, Coca-Cola, and others have made massive investments in China. Japanese companies have invested heavily in South Asia. The emergence of the European Union has given a new role to governments as builders of community and facilitators of trade and other economic activity.

## The Emergence of Environmentalism and Other Social Values

The past ten years have also brought an increasing awareness of the fact that we have not been very good stewards of the planet Earth.

Newspapers are filled with pictures of the latest environmental disaster, from oil spills to smog-filled cities. Scientists disagree about many of the facts, but they do agree that such issues as global warming and the production of greenhouse gases, the destruction of tropical rainforests and biodiversity, and the overall health of the ecosystem are here to stay. In a world where markets are more open and governments are more liberalized, environmentalism must be built into the way we think about business. It cannot be an afterthought, because the issues are too large and the consequences are potentially too large.

Environmentalism reinforces the idea that markets are global, since the big issues like global warming and biodiversity require sharing information and cooperation across traditional national boundaries. The mere existence of the Kyoto Treaty on global climate change is testament to the impact that environmentalism has had on modern life.

In some industries, environmentalism has literally changed the basis of competition. While some companies have adopted a "wait until all the facts are in" approach, others have used all of their political muscle to lobby against environmental laws and treaties. 3M created its Pollution Prevention Pays program in which they have tried to turn waste streams into products. DuPont, long seen as a large polluter by environmentalists, has committed to zero pollution. Even General Electric is getting in on the act, seeing environmentalism as a valuable way to think about innovation. Its "eco-imagination" campaign seeks to integrate thinking about the environment with thinking about the rest of its business.

In addition to environmentalism, we have seen an increasing public awareness of the impact that business has on society at large. The idea of social investing is a fast-growing segment of the investment industry, wherein companies are screened for the impact that they have on society. Mutual funds have been built on the idea of investing only in socially responsible companies. Protestors have emerged to criticize what they call "global capitalism" and its effects on local communities.

Large international coordinating bodies like the World Trade Organization and the International Monetary Fund have come under heavy fire for ignoring the effects of their economic policies on local communities and cultures.

## The Explosion of Information Technology

Certainly the liberalization of both markets and political institutions, and to some extent environmentalism and other social values, are dependent on the growth of information technology. Today's world is connected, wireless, plugged in, and turned on. The Internet is the hottest marketing tool in years, and the growth of smaller yet faster computers that can communicate with each other continues to fuel the information revolution.

The information revolution has decentralized the processing of information, and at the same time it has made it possible to link the decentralized processing into powerful networks. Applications like Microsoft Net Meeting and Lotus Notes, as well as e-mail in general, are more than "killer apps." They represent new modes of working, the consequences of which we have yet to understand. It is difficult to imagine an airport today without executives hunched over their PDAs, connected to their offices no matter where they are in the world.

Managers can get information on the results of a decision, indeed on performance, immediately, without waiting for the centralized information system to kick out a monthly report. Companies can almost instantly know buying patterns of their customers and potential customers, targeting markets more specifically. Web site developers can even look and see the kinds of Web sites that a particular computer user likes to "hit," compiling vast arrays of information from the so-called cookies file.

Executives like Bob Collingwood can go to a hotel in Jakarta, turn on CNN, plug in their computers, and fax and e-mail to their hearts' content. There is no technological reason to ever be out of touch with "the office." Indeed the very idea of "the office" is fast becoming antiquated.

## CHANGES IN PRIMARY BUSINESS RELATIONSHIPS

These four dominant trends have had profound impacts on the primary business relationships. Managing these relationships using the managerial view won't work anymore. Its assumptions of stability and order are simply irrelevant.

### Customers

The traditional business mindset makes a customer a stakeholder with high importance. However, the traditional view that there is a tradeoff between price and performance, the only variables that really count, has become rapidly outdated. Customer interests can no longer be traded off with shareholder interests through the price-performance tradeoff. The lesson of the 1980s was that superior quality and low price have to go together. Toyota provided an object lesson to the American automobile industry that price and quality were a false tradeoff. In the 1990s superior service was added to the equation. Companies like Dell customized their production and service to bypass traditional industry bottlenecks. In the twenty-first century "speed" and "on demand" are key expectations of consumers. Amazon and Google epitomize companies whose business models are built on price, quality, service, and speed going together. Today's companies must deliver on all of these variables, and make money by doing so.

Companies such as L. L. Bean, American Express, Nordstrom, and Honda have raised the service bar for everyone. Businesses, especially small ones, that have enjoyed a historical advantage because of location are severely impacted by the existence of new technology. Local, independent bookstores have to serve customers better than the giants like

Barnes and Noble and Borders, and they have to be better than Amazon, which can deliver virtually any book, has little if any inventory, and is accessible twenty-four hours a day. All are competing on price, quality, service, and speed, which the customer demands.

When a customer calls American Express to dispute a charge and is treated in a respectful manner, and American Express investigates the facts and gets back to the customer with any questions or explanations, that customer begins to expect that level of service from other institutions, such as banks and car dealerships. Wal-Mart's continual focus on meeting customer needs of everyday low prices and friendly service has had profound effects on competitors in the retailing business.

### Suppliers

Under the old mindset, suppliers were "just somebody to buy stuff from."[4] As with the customer relationship, there was an assumption that price and performance were the variables that one used to make purchasing decisions, and that there was a tradeoff. Squeeze suppliers, and shareholders could do better. Suppliers could be pitted against each other to ensure that a company got the absolute rock-bottom price.

All of that has changed. Today the new information technology makes possible the interweaving of supplier and customer systems. Point-of-sale information technology and just-in-time inventory systems can be relayed back to the supplier's factory so that shelves, not inventory, can be replenished immediately without anyone bearing the cost of inventory.

The supplier relationship has also changed with regard to certification and liability. ISO 9000's program to certify attention to quality and ISO 14000's program to certify best practices with regard to environmental management are both sources of competitive advantage. No one wants to accept materials or services from a supplier that have been created in an environmentally dangerous way. Liability does not stop at the point of sale. The chain works backward to the source and forward to the deep pockets. In short, the traditional "value chain" has turned into a "responsibility chain."

Nike discovered the power of the responsibility chain when NGOs criticized the labor practices of the factories that supply Nike with products. Nike does not own these factories, but the fact that some of them employed child labor led to protests against Nike. Nike had to rethink its supplier relationships from start to finish.

We can no longer understand suppliers as "just someone to buy stuff from." Suppliers are more like partners today. If a business is global, it sometimes wants to deal with companies who can supply it globally. The trend is moving to deal with fewer suppliers, where trust and partnership are the watchwords rather than price and performance. Everyone has to have high quality and low prices in order to play. Suppliers are increasingly distinguished by service built on trust and partnership.

One of the most important developments of the last decade, supply-chain management, is built on the idea of more closely integrating the supplier-producer-customer chain. Under some scenarios, data entered at the retail level flow back through a producer to suppliers of that producer. New information technology has produced some sophisticated systems that weld together the interests of these stakeholder groups. Managing these groups and issues in the old managerial and production mode simply won't work in today's world.

### Employees

During the heyday of managerialism, employees could count on a stable relationship with their businesses. In return for doing a good job and loyalty, employees received good wages and benefits and an implicit promise that the company would take care of them. The stereotype of this relationship was portrayed in novels like Sloan Wilson's *The Man in the Gray Flannel Suit.* Today's typical employee, if there is such a person, is neither a man nor dressed in gray flannel. Furthermore, the old social contract (do your job and the company will take care of you) has been restructured.

The wave of business reengineering and restructuring that emerged in the 1990s and continues today has led to thousands of layoffs of employees who were doing their jobs. As one manager remarked to us, "It's tough to fire people, but when they simply aren't performing you see the need to do it. However, walking into a room with five hundred people who are doing their jobs well and firing them because you're restructuring the work—that's really hard."

The restructuring of work sometimes simply eliminated the need for employees or sometimes contracted jobs out in a less expensive manner. Spurred by global competitiveness and the new information technology, companies redesigned key processes to be more focused on customers, eliminating many bureaucratic practices. Indeed, the restructuring of work has entered the political arena in most Western countries; "outsourcing" has become a hot political issue, especially around election time. This issue cannot be addressed purely in the economic terms of the managerial view, at least not without understanding the political and social fallout that is likely to occur.

The best that can be said today is that the employment contract is for employability rather than continued employment. The best companies have realized that if they give employees challenging assignments and training in the skills necessary to be successful, then they have made their employees more employable, even though it might be with another firm.

In the same time frame, in the United States, many more women joined the workforce. Companies began to notice that the managerial view implicitly assumed that the typical employee was the sole wage earner for his family and was for the most part both white and male. This implicit view simply doesn't fit the new corporation with its diverse set of employees.

Diversity, managing diversity, and valuing diversity have become central ideas in understanding how companies manage the employee relationship. While each of these terms can mean many things, the basic idea is to question the assumptions about the structure of work. Enabling employees who are different from each other to work more effectively is the goal. Key differences are race, gender, sexual orientation, age, education, and culture (fueled again by the globalization phenomenon). All of these differences are capable of yielding both conflict and opportunity in the workplace of the twenty-first century. The old assumptions just don't apply.

### Financiers

You only have to open the newspaper to find out how the business relationship with financiers has changed. There are clarion calls for transparency in the wake of the Enron, Arthur Andersen, Tyco, Adelphia, and WorldCom scandals. Even the U.S. President has issued a call for more corporate integrity in financial reporting. In reality the model of shareholders as owning the firm that stands at the center of the managerial model has become enormously more complex. Michael Milken created debt that looked like equity. Enron pioneered the use of limited partnerships that were "off the books." Long-Term Capital Management pushed the limits of hedging and derivatives. While some of these examples pushed beyond the acceptable rules, the damage was elsewhere. The idea that shareholders have a special place at the center of the managerial model is an idea whose time has come and gone. There are multiple ways to finance the modern corporation, from equity to debt, to debt that looks like equity, to derivatives to hedge investments, to multiple ways to securitize the assets of the firm.

Bob Collingwood as CEO will have to worry about creditors, banks, shareholders, investment bankers, and more. The scandals have yielded a deep skepticism on the part of others that this complex financial process has any integrity at all. The immediate response to the scandals at the beginning of the twenty-first century was to pass a piece of legislation in the United States, the Sarbanes-Oxley Act of 2002, or Sarbox. Crafted in the wake of the revelations at Enron, this legislation requires companies to prove that all of their processes that report financial results meet the government's rules. While some of these reforms have helped companies become more transparent, it has made it much more difficult to find accounting and auditing services, and some have estimated a doubling and tripling of the costs. Furthermore, the scandals continue at such companies as HealthSouth and AIG.

Many have argued that business has lost the public trust, especially in the United States. In a recent survey of CEOs, the Business Roundtable Institute for Corporate Ethics found that CEOs believed that the number-one ethics issue facing business executives was the loss of the public trust, fueled by all of the recent scandals.[5] New regulatory regimes have been implemented, a new accounting board established in the United States, but the conversation continues about whether or not business can be left to its own to govern itself, in light of the financial scandals.

We believe that this problem has emerged largely because we have relied on an outmoded model of value creation and trade: the managerial view, with shareholders at the center.

## Communities

The idea that business should be a good citizen in the local community is an old idea. In the past this often meant obeying the law, donating to the United Way or other charities, or sending employees to help out in schools and other nonprofit organizations. Today things are more complicated.

First of all, the very idea of community has gotten more complex. The traditional notion of community is about a particular geographical place—a physical community where people make their lives. Community still retains that connotation of place, but it has been broadened to include the "community of interest" or "virtual community," and these ideas may require a great deal more of businesses. Communities of interest and virtual communities have used the power of the Internet and information technology to expand their reach beyond geography. Companies have to take an active role in deciding which communities they are a part of, and how they are going to make those communities better off.

Second, in a relatively free society, companies ignore communities at their peril. The political process is fairly open and easy to use, at least in terms of getting the news of one's interests out into cyberspace. Local, geographically based communities pass laws designed to favor or deter particular companies like Wal-Mart, while communities of interest band together to lobby at a national and international level.

Indeed, part of the business reform movement of the past decade has focused on new understandings of the idea of business citizenship. Much work has been done at the United Nations and other NGOs to develop sets of global principles of conduct for multinational companies. Many of these proposals for reform do adopt the language of stakeholders, but unfortunately they do not always exhibit the kind of comprehensive view that we outline in this book. Stakeholders are identified with communities rather than customers, suppliers, employees, financiers, and communities. These proposals often focus too much on one stakeholder (community or environment) and juxtapose the interests of community with the interests of shareholders. These reforms are themselves caught squarely in the middle of the managerial view. Seeing community and shareholder interests as conflicting is likely, in our view, to lead executives astray. The point is that we need to make it a part of the ordinary everyday life of managers to figure out how to satisfy shareholders and communities at the same time.

CHANGES IN SECONDARY BUSINESS RELATIONSHIPS

The shifts in markets, political institutions, environmental and other social values, and information technology have also caused changes in what we have called the instrumental environment of a firm. In some cases, such as activist groups, new stakeholders have arisen, and in others, such as governments, there is a different kind of importance attached to that group. The managerial view with its obsession with shareholder value at the center is incapable of understanding these profound changes since it relies on stability, predictability, and a more orderly process of change.

## Government

Even with the liberalization of political institutions, government still has an enormous effect on business. With the globalization of markets, it is more imperative than ever to make government a part of the mindset for managers. Government in the twenty-first century is really "governments" as there are a host of individual groups and agencies who make up government for today's corporation. Figure 2.3 shows a more detailed stakeholder map of government. Government officials, elected and appointed, understand that capitalism and business are the engines that lead to prosperity and growth; therefore the awareness of the reciprocal effects of business and government has been heightened. Public officials have been routinely elected on the promise of curtailing this role and seeking a return to letting markets operate. Today with the lack of public trust, public officials are running for office on such issues as "stopping Wal-Mart," "executive compensation," and "having business pay for health care."

The business-government relationship in the United States has been founded on the principle of the watchdog—that is, the legitimate role of government is to regulate business in the public interest and to enforce

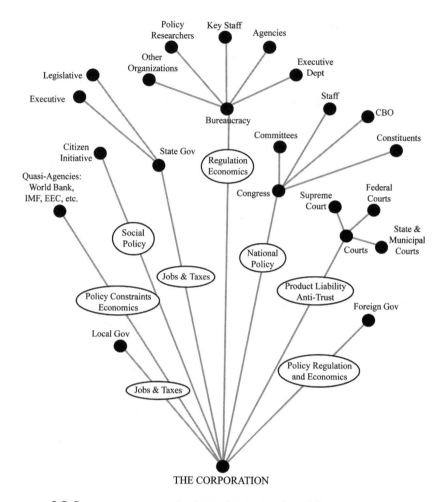

2.3. Business-government relationship in the United States

strict antitrust laws to ensure adherence to market principles. The recent accounting scandals have reopened the issue of the proper role of government regulation in ensuring the transparency and basic ethics of the market.

The issues here are far from settled, and political scientists and policy makers continue to debate cause and effect. From the standpoint of the executive, these repartees miss the major issue: how to manage in a world where there are multiple influences from various levels of government, or more properly from governments, and where the corporation and its managers can in turn affect the direction of public policy and government action. A necessary condition for solving this problem is to understand the interactions that are possible among business and various government actors. Government is not a monolithic entity, and it does not exist in a vacuum. Agencies, congressional committees, presidential commissions, and presidential staff members are all susceptible to multiple influences. Yet the U.S. federal bureaucracy is a large and fragmented entity. Multiply these effects for Bob Collingwood as he operates in a global environment with many different forms of government.

Additionally, there are many quasi-agencies that affect business, such as the World Bank, the IMF, the U.N., and the WTO. These organizations are themselves complex global entities, and they sometimes propose policy constraints—for example, by de facto determining the amount of credit available to some countries to purchase goods and services.

The Congress considers several thousand pieces of legislation every session, some of which can have drastic effects on businesses. In addition, national policy changes, such as tax and depreciation schedules, capital formation incentives, and the creation of new forms of regulation affect the business community as a whole, even if the marginal effect on a single firm is slight. Hence, today's CEO must spend a good deal of time and resources deciding how to contribute to the conversation about public policy legislation in Congress.

State governments offer a different set of issues for management, and these issues vary from region to region. Companies that operate on a national scale often find themselves with numerous sets of regulations. Most national breweries, for example, ship to multiple states from large regional breweries, yet tax and packaging requirements vary from state to state, even to the kind of packaging that is permissible. State legislatures consider several hundred thousand pieces of legislation every session, and the resources expended just to stay informed, much less to try to actively participate, are enormous. The courts offer yet another source of government influence on business. The old model of the elementary civics books with the separation of executive, legislative, and judicial branches of government simply does not apply to today's world. From historic products-liability decisions and equal opportunity cases to anti-trust issues, the courts at the state and federal levels can affect the nature of business.

We need only think about the tobacco or pharmaceutical businesses or Microsoft or AT&T to see the influence of the courts on the modern corporation. General Electric's failure to convince European regulators of the good sense of its merger with Honeywell (and Allied Signal) stands as a testament to the power of this multitude of influences on business that must become part and parcel of the executive's mindset, not as an add-on to thinking about shareholder value but as a necessary part of how shareholder value, and stakeholder value more generally, gets created in the twenty-first century.

The point is that not any one government or piece of government can affect a firm but rather, when taken in conjunction, the cumulative effect is enormous. To properly manage the primary relationships with customers, suppliers, employees, communities, and financiers, executives like Bob Collingwood must spend time and resources understanding and dealing with governments in a strategic fashion.

## Competitors

Competition has been the cornerstone of our system of managerial capitalism. Until relatively recently, however, U.S. businesses have not had to deal with powerful competitors from other countries. In the 1950s "made in Japan" meant "junk" or "cheap" or some such derogatory term, while in the 1980s it was perceived as the hallmark of quality. Even with the downfall of the Japanese economy in the late 1990s,

Japanese companies are still formidable competitors, in part because they are global. Honda is in Marysville, Ohio. Toyota is in Tennessee. General Motors owns part of Isuzu, a Japanese firm. IBM's personal computer business is owned jointly by IBM and Chinese investors. Service calls to traditional American firms may be routed to India. In many hospitals in the United States, the technicians in the hospital take the X-rays or CAT scans, then transmit them over the Internet to be read and interpreted by doctors in India. There are no longer clear national boundaries, and the effects on those companies who assume that such boundaries give level playing fields are disastrous. There is competition from abroad in almost every formerly U.S.-dominant industry.

The rules are different today. There is no level playing field and no stability that comes with such a field. Firms compete globally, but they compete locally as well. Companies have to match the scale and scope of other global competitors and they must also match the local market knowledge of local competitors.

In part, the emergence of global competition is what makes the necessity to abandon the dominant managerial view of the firm so urgent. As long as all significant competition is domestic, everyone must play by the same rules. Each competitor bears the burden and shares the benefits of government, whether corrupt or clean, a fickle consumer population, environmentalists, and so on. There is an umbrella effect by which firms in an industry can implicitly or explicitly coordinate their response to various issues. No one is at a competitive disadvantage; hence, everyone can afford to proceed as if the managerial view were still appropriate. When nondomestic competitors, who may have grown up with a different set of cultural rules and institutions, figure out how to satisfy customers and government with high-quality products that are less expensive and meet all requirements, then the umbrella folds. This scenario has already taken place in industry after industry around the world.

## Consumer Advocates

Much has happened since the early 1960s when President Kennedy announced the Consumer Bill of Rights, beginning the modern consumer movement. Consumer advocates today affect almost every industry involved in consumer goods marketing. Most executives are familiar with the story of Ralph Nader and General Motors' Corvair, which resulted in national prominence for Nader and the end of a product line for GM. Activists have taken on other industries from pharmaceuticals and infant formula to utilities, many perhaps spurred by Nader's original success.

Many successful companies recognize the importance of the consumer movement. Procter and Gamble expends a great deal of resources handling consumer complaints, as do other top retailers like Nordstrom and L. L. Bean. Many consumer leaders want change in the marketplace. They know that, if necessary, government can be brought into the picture. The cost ultimately would be borne by the consumer, however, through either higher taxes or higher product costs. Therefore, these leaders are amenable to real voluntarism, and to negotiation outside the formal arena of government.

## Environmentalists

Another outgrowth of the turbulent 1960s is the concern with environmental quality: clean air, water, and land, as well as conservation of natural resources. The environmental movement has roots that are as old as the pioneers, with some prominent organizations like the Sierra Club having been around since the 1890s, but several events in the 1960s heightened the consciousness of many members of the public and gave rise to the environmental advocacy groups that many executives now face.

More than forty years of environmental regulation at multiple levels of government have given a renewed importance to working with environmental groups on a voluntary basis. We have begun to see joint business and environmentalist partnerships where environmentalists help companies tackle problems from pollution to global warming. Once again, this is not an "add-on" to thinking about shareholders but a key ingredient in the creation of value for all of the key stakeholders. In the twenty-first century businesses must become both green and profitable.

### Special-Interest Groups

A more general phenomenon underlies the shifts in the business world engendered by government, foreign competition, consumer advocates, and environmentalists: the concern with non governmental organizations (NGOs) or special-interest groups (SIGs). The idea behind NGOs is that a group or individual can use the political process to further a position on a particular issue, such as globalization, outsourcing, AIDS, abortion, women's rights, prayer in schools, or any of hundreds of other issues. The problem that NGOs represent for the manager is that one can never be sure that an ad hoc group will not form to oppose the company on any particular issue.

Special-interest politics is not a new phenomenon. Changes in modern communications technology, however, make it especially important for managers to be aware of the agendas of interest groups. Organized protest groups can attract media attention nationwide and can use the political process to their advantage. Thus, the ability of business managers to respond to a variety of issues and events is crucial to success in industries that are vulnerable to criticism by special-interest groups.

Today's managers need theories and realistic help in dealing with NGOs and SIGs as they affect their businesses. In particular, they need to take this change into account when setting their business strategy.

## Media

Little stirs anger in an executive more than an "unfair" story in the press. When one's company or products, or even one's character, has been attacked in a forum where there is little chance of reply, the feeling of anger quickly turns to helplessness. It is easy to wake up in a cold sweat from a nightmare of the 60 Minutes crew showing up unannounced at your corporate headquarters to investigate the latest consumer or employee complaint. Or, suppose you find a Web site that is solely devoted to showing how your company is the most evil one on the face of the earth. Credible blogs are important new tools for marketing, and they can be deadly when critical of a company.

Mass communications technology has indeed changed the role of the media with regard to business. More than ever, large organizations live in a fishbowl with their every action open to some form of public scrutiny. The media represents another form of change for the executive who wishes to succeed in today's environment.

### THE NEED FOR A FRAMEWORK

The combination of the four macro trends, the shifts in primary stakeholder relationships, and the emergence of pressures on these relationships from others in the environment is too much for the managerial model with shareholders at the center. The single-minded focus on shareholder value encourages executives to ignore these changes and stakeholders regardless of the consequences. We need a new approach— a conceptual shift—a new way to make sense of business so that all of this change doesn't seem extraordinary.

An analogy may help. Suppose that you make a New Year's resolution to do a better job of cleaning up your office. You buy a file drawer and construct a set of categories into which you file all of your important papers, memos, and reports. Each file is carefully labeled. Let us suppose that you are religious in your zeal to keep your desk clean and your papers filed. You find that your system works quite well for some time, but you notice that as time passes the file labeled "Miscellaneous" keeps getting larger and larger. You have to add new files with new categories, some of which overlap the old set of categories. Cross-referencing becomes such a nightmare that you and your assistant finally give up. Furthermore, you find that some of your files are no longer used. You make very few additions or deletions to these old files, and you find that much of the information that you need to make a decision or get something accomplished comes from a variety of different files. Nothing ever seems to be in a convenient place. If these problems are left unsolved, pretty soon your filing system becomes a mess. You can't find anything important anymore. Your files have become an effective way of dealing with the past, but not the present and future. Your desk soon reassumes its cluttered look and you must make another effort to start over at the New Year.

What went wrong? Your filing system became obsolete as changes took place in the world around you. Patching up the system by adding a few new files worked for a while, but eventually the whole file drawer needed to be rethought, and a newer, more appropriate set of files and categories needed to be established. In short, you were in need of a conceptual revolution—a change in mindset.

Bob Collingwood and his colleagues in the modern business corporation are in the same boat. Their tendency is to respond in a piecemeal fashion that minimizes the trouble of a particular issue. They are not encouraged to embrace the changes and the stakeholders, and find new ways to create value in these demands for conflicting aims. Focusing on minimizing the harm to shareholders from environmental regulation simply asks the wrong question with respect to how to make products and services better, so that they are clean, green, and profitable. The companies who embrace stakeholder conflict in the twenty-first century and find a way to create value for conflicting stakeholder interests will be the winners.

In short, we need new concepts, new conceptual filing systems, that reorient our way of looking at the world to encompass present and future changes. We want to suggest that the idea of the managerial model with shareholders at the center needs to be dropped in favor of a better, more robust view: the managing for stakeholders view.

# The Basic Framework

As soon as the plane touched down and taxied to the gate, Bob Collingwood turned on his Blackberry. He had twenty-three new e-mail messages, none of them particularly urgent. His marketing and finance people were evidently having a battle over how to price a new product. The finance people wanted relatively higher prices so that there would be less pressure on earnings, while the marketing people wanted a lower price to increase sales. The government relations people were getting in on the act, since the environmental impact of the new product was not yet proven, and they were fearful that an early release might spur some critics to offer restrictive legislation in a couple of states. Bob's public relations person requested a meeting to go over the company's policy on corporate giving, and whether it should continue to encourage employees to make unrestricted contributions to charities of their choice (which the company matched) or become more restricted.

There was also an e-mail from the training and development people lauding a new business bestseller on "strategy execution," with a proposal to invite the authors to give a presentation at the company's leadership development seminar. Maybe a leadership development seminar was what the team needed, and maybe the team needed to execute its plans better and faster. But Bob suspected something else was wrong. There would be twenty-three more e-mails after the next leg of the trip. Many of them would outline the tradeoffs that had to be made between shareholders and customers, employees and suppliers, or communities, customers, and shareholders. Bob had to figure out some way to escape the tradeoff thinking that was restricting the creativity of his people.

### THE BASIC FRAMEWORK: A SIMPLE IDEA

Implicit in our critique of the managerial model with shareholders at the center has been our reliance on the idea of stakeholders. Stakeholders are the groups that can affect or be affected by the achievement of a business's core purpose. The idea is a simple one. A business is successful insofar as it creates value for and satisfies key stakeholders continually over time. It must be aware of potential influences from groups that may be at odds with its purpose. At the very heart of the process of value creation that is business, we find a profound concern with stakeholder interests and relationships.

For most businesses, managers or entrepreneurs must put together a deal (or agreement, or contract) so that customers, employees, suppliers, financiers, and communities share jointly in the value that gets created. Over time, the function of the executive is to balance the interests of these groups, to increase the value that gets created for all of them, and to keep their interests and desires headed roughly in the same direction. We believe that if Bob Collingwood and his colleagues adopt such a "managing for stakeholders" approach they will have a much easier time creating value for stakeholders simultaneously. Some examples may be helpful.

EXAMPLES OF CREATING VALUE FOR STAKEHOLDERS

Patricia is a manager of ABC Pharma. She is responsible for a project that works on diabetes. She must deal simultaneously with employees who are doing the research, potential customers (including a chain of wholesalers, retailers, agents, agencies, and the medical community), suppliers of chemicals, testing agents, and the like. She has to be cognizant of the interests of financiers as well as the community, which is fairly well understood in this instance due to the intrusive nature of state intervention in the pharmaceutical industry. If she is successful, she will get all of these diverse interests going in roughly the same direction over time. Sometimes she will have to trade one off against the other, but she must discover a way to make them work together.

Jennifer had an idea to start a catalog company that offered automobile radio and stereo equipment. To do so she had to negotiate arrangements with a host of suppliers, find lists of potential customers, hire employees to design catalogs, fill orders, and deal with customer questions, as well as continually meet with the banks and family members that provided the original financing. As the business grew she had to negotiate a land deal to build a warehouse. This involved a number of permits from agencies and visits to neighboring parcels of land to talk about water usage, potential environmental problems, and other social issues. If Jennifer was successful, it was because she managed to put together a deal so that all of these stakeholders were winners over time. In the beginning suppliers and financiers may well have been most important, and it may be that communities became important only later. But, if Jennifer's company is to be sustainable, all stakeholder relationships have to push in roughly the same direction.

Rinaldo and his friends have an idea for a new computer game. One friend is a very good programmer. Rinaldo's expertise is in getting a team of people to work together. He gathers together a team with differing sources of expertise, puts together a business plan, and finds some funding from venture capitalists and another small computer-game startup. Initially Rinaldo will have to focus on keeping the team engaged in what they are doing and managing the expectations of the financiers. But soon will come the time to beta test the product, and potential customers will be needed. Eventually, if successful, Rinaldo will have to worry about getting a supplier to manufacture the finished product. And, given the current arrangement of social institutions, Rinaldo will have to worry about how the game is viewed by the broader community. For instance, if the game is about how teenagers can commit more juvenile delinquency, there may well be a move to boycott the game or label it as unsuitable for minors.

In all three of these examples, entrepreneurs, both startup and existing venture entrepreneurs, have to become enmeshed and engaged in stakeholder relationships. They have to solve conflicts while preserving the joint nature of these relationships. They have to be responsible for the effects of their actions, if they want their ventures to survive. They have to understand that employees, customers, and other stakeholders are complex beings, and that they cannot manage with a "one size fits all" point of view. They have to understand that the interests of one group cannot always be traded off against the interests of shareholders. Competitors are important to understand. They play a role when a company is unable to continue to create maximum value for its stakeholders.

Shareholders are one very important stakeholder, but there are others. We want to suggest that there are at least two important kinds. First, as these examples make plain, there are stakeholders that we might call *primary* or *definitional stakeholders* to signify that they are vital to the continued growth and survival of any business. Specifically, these are customers, employees, suppliers, communities, and financiers. Take away the support of any one of these groups, and the resulting business is not sustainable. This is perhaps less clear in the case of community, but remember that in a relatively free society, if community interests aren't satisfied, then activists go to government for relief, and the result

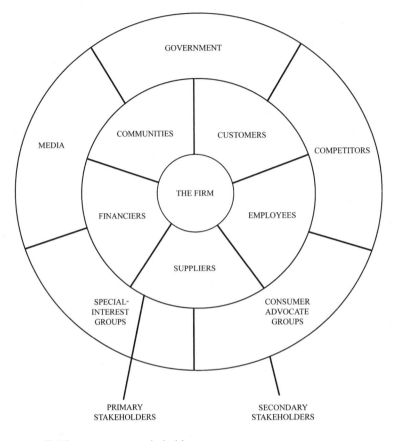

3.1. Basic two-tier stakeholder map

is more and more regulation that may well threaten the enterprise. Second, we need to look at the broader business environment on a routine basis, and in particular we have to be concerned with those groups that can affect our primary relationships. We'll call these groups *secondary stakeholders*. So, activists, governments, competitors, media, environmentalists, corporate critics, and special-interest groups are all stakeholders, at least instrumentally, insofar as they can affect the primary business relationships. Figure 3.1 shows where these two kinds of stakeholders fit into the overall scheme.

SOME GUIDING PRINCIPLES

While the idea of stakeholders provides a good organizing framework, it is incomplete without some guiding principles to help managers apply it to the real world of business. In later chapters we will have more specific ideas about how to apply the stakeholder framework. These guiding principles come from our experience with many companies and represent the stakeholder mindset that is necessary if the framework is to be workable.

1. *Stakeholder interests go together over time.* The very idea of managing for stakeholders is predicated on the fact that the process of value creation is about finding the intersection of interests for primary stakeholders. Value creation is a joint process that makes each primary stakeholder better off. Bob Collingwood's company's products and services must create value for customers, first and foremost, so that they are willing to pay for them. Suppliers must be willing to do business with Woodland International, so that products and services can be created in the first place, and if the suppliers are committed to making Woodland even more effective and productive, then both will be winners. Woodland must offer employees jobs (wages and benefits) that are acceptable, and if Bob and his colleagues can get employees to share the purpose of Woodland, to come to work engaged and ready to create value, then all will be winners. Woodland needs to be a good citizen in the communities in which it operates, if for no other reason than that in a relatively free and open society, citizens can use the political process to force Woodland to be a better citizen. If Woodland acts as a responsible citizen, it may well generate very positive good will and be able to operate more freely. Finally, Woodland needs to show returns to its shareholders, meet obligations to debt holders, banks, and others. Profits shouldn't cause conflict with other stakeholders; they are the scorecard that tells us how well we are managing the whole set of stakeholder relationships. Bob and his colleagues must keep

these stakeholder interests in balance, hopefully mutually reinforcing one another.

2. *We need to find solutions to issues that satisfy multiple stakeholders simultaneously.* Bob Collingwood's problem is that his world is fragmented. Issues and problems come at him and his team from lots of places, in lots of forms. He could spend his entire job just talking to customers, or employees. He needs to find a way to develop programs, policies, strategies, even products and services that satisfy multiple stakeholders simultaneously. The first step in that process is to recognize that he needs to look for simultaneous solutions. For instance, suppose that he is under pressure to make a particular service more affordable to low-income citizens. Under the managerial view with shareholders at the center, he might see this as an illegitimate "tax on shareholders." Such a view would constrain innovation and cause constant friction with critics and regulators. He might take this criticism as a call for innovation and productivity, so that if he can figure something out, he can develop a new market (lower-income customers), satisfy some critics, and become a good citizen in the community. The difference in mindsets is fairly substantial, and so will be the search for a solution.

3. *Everything that we do serves stakeholders. We never trade off the interests of one versus the other continuously over time.* Just as many successful companies think in terms of how to serve the customer or how to serve the employees, it is possible to generalize this philosophy to how to serve stakeholders. The "reason for being" for most organizations is that they serve some need in their external environment. When an organization loses its sense of purpose and mission, when it focuses itself internally on the needs of its managers, it is in danger of becoming irrelevant. Someone else (if competition is possible) will serve the environmental need better. The more we can begin to think in terms of how to better serve stakeholders, the more likely we will be to survive and prosper over time. As we will suggest in the next chapter, a manag-

ing for stakeholders approach asks the company to clearly articulate how its basic business proposition makes its stakeholders better off.

One of Bob Collingwood's problems is that he is sorely tempted to make tradeoffs among stakeholders. And, while inevitably there must sometimes be tradeoffs, he should be very cautious. Keeping all primary stakeholder interests going in the same direction is more difficult. Much innovative work has been done in this area, as companies have put together the interests of suppliers and customers in new methods of supply-chain management. Indeed some companies have added the interests of communities as they have built environmentally friendly processes into their supply chain processes. Thinking about all five primary stakeholders leads to innovation and growth, while thinking in terms of tradeoffs leads to stagnation and business as usual.

Sometimes tradeoffs have to be made in the real world of business. When executives have to make tradeoffs, however, they need to take the next step and ask how the tradeoffs can be improved for both stakeholders, or to continue to ask how a company can innovate to get these interests going in the same direction. Tradeoff thinking is easy and fatal.

4. *We act with purpose that fulfills our commitment to stakeholders. We act with aspiration toward fulfilling our dreams and theirs.* We believe that the key idea that holds this stakeholder mindset together is the idea that businesses can have a purpose. There are few limits on the kinds of purpose that can drive a business. Wal-Mart may stand for "everyday low prices." Merck can stand for alleviating human suffering. Novo Nordisk stands for eliminating diabetes. The point is that if an entrepreneur or an executive can find a purpose that speaks to the hearts and minds of key stakeholders, it is more likely that there will be sustained success.

Purpose is complex. Running a purposeful business is even more complicated. In Chapter 4 we will say more about the complexities of purpose-oriented thinking, which we shall call "enterprise strategy" or "enterprise thinking." Once we give up the idea of the managerial view with shareholders in the center as the only possible framework for a business, the field is wide open. Perhaps maximizing shareholder value is a good purpose for a business, but surely it's not the only one.

Purpose is inspirational. The Grameen Bank wants to eliminate poverty. Fannie Mae wants to make housing affordable to every income level in society. The local restaurant Tastings wants to bring really good food and wine to lots of people in the community. All of these organizations have to generate profits, or else they cannot pursue their purposes. We can't emphasize this idea too much. Capitalism works because we can pursue our purpose with others. When we coalesce around a big idea, or a joint purpose evolves from our day-to-day activities with each other, then great things can happen.

5. *We need to have a philosophy of voluntarism—to actively engage stakeholders and manage the relationships ourselves, rather than leaving it to government.* When executives and pundits are committed to the managerial view with shareholders at the center, there is a temptation to look at the myriad stakeholder pressures and play "Blame the Stakeholder." We have argued that the real problem here is our mindset. In short, we have met the enemy, and he is us. The challenge for us is to reorient our thinking and our managerial processes to be responsive to stakeholders. We believe that such a stakeholder mindset must be based on the ideas of voluntarism and engagement. Voluntarism means that an organization must of its own will undertake to satisfy its key stakeholders. A situation where a solution to a stakeholder problem is imposed by a government agency or the courts must be seen as a managerial failure. Similarly, a situation where Firm A satisfies the needs of consumer advocates, government agencies, and so on better than Firm B must be seen as a competitive loss by Firm B. The driving force of an organization becomes, under a voluntarism philosophy of management, to create as much value for stakeholders as possible. Voluntarism is

impossible without engagement. All of the management team, indeed all employees at Woodland, must come to see their jobs as inherently creating value for all stakeholders.

6. *We need intensive communication and dialogue with stakeholders— not just those who are friendly.* Obviously we need intensive dialogue through multiple methods with customers, suppliers, employees, and shareholders, but communities, critics, and other secondary stakeholders count as well. Critics are especially important dialogue members. Critics are trying to give Bob and his team another point of view about Woodland International. One way to see critics is as representing unmet market needs, since the critic wants the company to act differently. It is the job of the executives to see if there is some underlying business model, so that this unmet need can be turned into an entrepreneurial opportunity creating wins for all stakeholders. Not every critic can be satisfied, not every critic has a legitimate point of view, and not every need can be met. But too often executives don't meet with their critics enough to determine whether or not there is an opportunity to create value. Dialogue is the foundation of a free society, and the foundation of capitalism itself. Despite fictional stories about spot market transactions where every player just knows the prices, real business is built on a foundation of solid, honest, and open communication. Indeed, most management meetings we have been a part of for the past twenty-five years have all, at some point, reinforced the need for better communication. This is also true in the managing for stakeholders view—satisfying the need is just more difficult and even more intense.

No one learned this lesson better than Shell Oil. It was hammered in the press and public when it seemingly did nothing to stop the death of activist Ken Sira-Wawi in Nigeria, and when it made the well-meaning and perhaps technically correct decision to sink the Brent Spar oil platform in the North Sea. Shell changed its approach to make stakeholder engagement a key business philosophy. It no longer gets surprised by outside stakeholders, and its executives are actively engaged with all of its stakeholders, both friends and critics.

7. *Stakeholders consist of real people with names and faces and children. They are complex.* Of course people are complex, and that should go without saying. However, much of the popular thinking about business people assumes just the opposite. We often make assumptions that business people are in it only for their own narrowly defined self-interest. One main assumption of the managerial view with shareholders at the center is that shareholders care only about returns, and therefore their agents, managers, should care only about returns. In the words of one CEO, "The only assets I manage go up and down the elevators every day."

Human beings are complicated. Most of us do what we do because we are self-interested and interested in others. Business works in part because of our urge to create things with others and for others. Working on a team or creating a new product or delivery mechanism that makes customers' lives better or happier or more pleasurable can be contributing factors to why we go to work each day. This is not to deny the economic incentive of getting a pay check. The assumption of narrow self-interest is extremely limiting and can be self-reinforcing—people can begin to act in a narrow, self-interested way if they believe that is what is expected of them, as some of the scandals, such as Enron, have shown. We need to be open to a more complex psychology—one any parent finds familiar after shepherding the growth and development of their children. We have encountered story after story where managers discovered that their adversaries were a lot more like them than they had originally thought. In short, they discovered that these adversaries shared a great deal of their own humanity: a lesson we should all remember.

8. *We need to generalize the marketing approach.* We need to "overspend" on understanding stakeholder needs, using marketing tech-

niques to segment stakeholders to provide a better understanding of their individual needs and using marketing research tools to understand the multi-attribute nature of most stakeholder groups. We might define "overspending" as paying extra attention, beyond that warranted by considerations of efficiency, to those groups who are critical for the long-term success of the firm. Overspending on stakeholders without whose support the company would fail can make sense in a number of ways.

For instance, many fast-moving consumer goods (FMCG) companies overspend on customers, interviewing several thousand a year. Telecom companies traditionally overspent on the attention they paid to the regulatory process, which was for a long time its major source of revenue. Oil companies should likewise consider adopting a conscious policy of overspending on OPEC as well as government and stakeholders who can convey a positive image to the public. Chemical companies have recently begun to overspend on environmentalists, trying to clean up their image as "dirty companies" and "spoilers of the environment." Overspending is not necessarily measured in monetary terms. Spending may be in terms of more time or more energy or whatever the relevant resource required by a given stakeholder group.

Applying the marketing approach has other benefits as well. By applying marketing principles we can understand stakeholder needs in a more detailed and fine-grained fashion. This leads to innovation and growth. Understanding customer needs in segments that are not currently being served can be a source of innovation. Likewise, understanding what critics are telling you about product defects can be a way to improve and develop new offerings. Stakeholders are a source of innovation and growth, but we must create "stakeholder-facing" organizations, much in the way that some have tried to create "customer-facing" organizations. In stakeholder-facing organizations every action is oriented toward understanding stakeholders and serving them better.

9. *We engage with both primary and secondary stakeholders.* The basic

idea behind the stakeholder approach is that if a group or individual can affect a company or be affected by a company, then there needs to be some interaction and some strategic thinking. Many executives get caught up in whether or not a particular stakeholder group, especially critics, are "legitimate" or not. While this is an important issue for some purposes, the stakeholder mindset encourages executives to meet, interact, and negotiate with both legitimate stakeholders, and those whose legitimacy may be questioned from an overall point of view.

In very practical terms, groups that have some power must be taken into account, regardless of whether or not in a pure capitalism system they should be there at all. In our relatively free and open society, the consequences of not negotiating with a broad range of stakeholders is that they use the political process to pressure government to enact a set of rules that is not likely to be optimal for company interests. You can think of this idea in terms of "managerial legitimacy"—that is, if a group has some power to affect the company, then it is legitimate to spend managerial time worrying about that group. Often, because these interactions start off with stereotypes of the behavior of both the business and the critic, careful attention to process (as we suggest in Chapter 5) can turn the relationship into one positive for both sides.

10. *We constantly monitor and redesign processes to make them better serve our stakeholders.* A hallmark of the stakeholder mindset is that in today's world no one gets it right all the time. Whatever your interactions and strategies are with stakeholders, they can always be improved. The classic case for such improvement comes from thinking about the environment. By paying attention to the environment, and environmentalists, companies from McDonald's to 3M have radically redefined their production processes to turn waste streams into new products, realize millions of dollars in cost savings, and gain a reputation as companies that are environmentally friendly and willing to work with environmental groups.

■ Box 3.1 Ten Principles of Managing for Stakeholders

1. Stakeholder interests need to go together over time.
2. We need to have a philosophy of voluntarism—to engage stakeholders and manage relationships ourselves, rather than leaving it to government.
3. We need to find solutions to issues that satisfy multiple stakeholders simultaneously.
4. Everything that we do serves stakeholders. We never trade off the interests of one versus the other continuously over time.
5. We act with purpose that fulfills our commitment to stakeholders. We act with aspiration towards fulfilling our dreams and theirs.
6. We need intensive communication and dialogue with stakeholders—not just those who are friendly.
7. Stakeholders consist of real people with names and faces and children. They are complex.
8. We need to generalize the marketing approach.
9. We engage with both primary and secondary stakeholders.
10. We constantly monitor and redesign processes to make them better serve our stakeholders.

APPLYING THE BASIC FRAMEWORK

We can apply the ten principles of the stakeholder framework and mindset at three levels in thinking about business. First, managing for stakeholders must make sense for the business as a whole. We need to understand who the critical stakeholders are for each business, and what their stakes are. Second, we must understand the business and managerial processes used either explicitly or implicitly to manage the relationships with key stakeholders. Finally, we need to understand the everyday interactions and transactions with stakeholders.

### The Business as a Whole: Mapping Stakeholders

Who are those groups and individuals who can affect and are affected by the achievement of an organization's purpose? How can we construct a "stakeholder map" of an organization? What are the problems in constructing such a map?

To be practical, the stakeholder framework must capture specific groups and individuals as stakeholders and must allow the adoption of an action orientation. It must be capable of yielding concrete actions with specific groups and individuals. "Managing for stakeholders," as a mindset, refers to the necessity for a business to manage the relationships with its specific stakeholder groups in an action-oriented way.

Stakeholders need to be identified at the generic level, as shown in Figure 3.1. In addition, they need to be identified at a finer level of analysis as well. So, for instance, it is insufficient, and frankly not very helpful, to identify "customers" as a key stakeholder, except when the firm is trying to develop an overall set of principles or values with respect to customers. We need to apply the principle of generalizing the marketing approach by segmenting stakeholders into more meaningful categories. A more helpful identification might be: (1) distributors (or distributors segmented by country, size, or other variable); (2) key retail accounts; and (3) end users (again by appropriate segment). Similarly, communities may be segmented in many different ways: (1) communities where we have plants; (2) communities where many of our employees live; (3) countries and communities where our products are sold. There is not one right way to identify stakeholders, but a meaningful stakeholder identification process can be undertaken so that the generic stakeholder map of Figure 3.1 can be turned into the more useful stakeholder map of Figure 3.2.

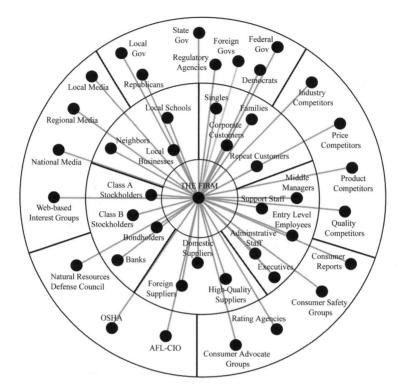

3.2. Specific stakeholder map for a typical company

Of course there might be different maps for different businesses in a multi-business firm. In such a firm, it is paramount to have a set of principles that ties together how the firm expects to treat its top-level definitional stakeholders, such as customers, suppliers, employees, communities, and financiers, since in today's very public business world there is some need for consistency.

We have depicted these stakeholder maps in diagrams showing the company in the middle. Since our emphasis is on managing for stakeholders as a way to think about management, such a depiction can be useful. It can, however, give the impression that the company is at the center of the universe, and this is misleading. We could look at the world from the viewpoint of any one stakeholder. We suggest in Chapter 5 that one technique for creating value for stakeholders is to see the world from their point of view. Put a key stakeholder in the middle and map their stakeholders. Indeed, Novo Nordisk draws their stakeholder map with customers and potential customers, or "people with diabetes," in the center of the map. Each company can create its own picture that is most useful to its unique purpose.

A number of successful companies are well known for their positions regarding stakeholders at this level of the company as a whole. H. B. Fuller lists customers as its most important stakeholder followed by employees, stockholders, and communities, in that order. Similarly, Johnson and Johnson's credo lists shareholders last, and customers first.

Figure 3.3 depicts how a specific stakeholder map could be turned into one that recognizes "names and faces."[1] Ultimately, stakeholder groups consist of real live human beings, and the information technology that we have today lets us take a personal approach to managing for stakeholders.

Box 3.2 shows an analysis of the stakes or interests of some of those specific stakeholder groups listed in the stakeholder map (Fig. 3.2). Figure 3.2 is actually a disguised stakeholder map for a company we shall call XYZ. The stake of XYZ's owners varied among specific stakeholder groups. Employees of XYZ, and the pension funds that own XYZ may be concerned with long-term growth of XYZ's stock. Their retirement income will depend on a healthy XYZ and its ability to earn returns during their retirement years. Other shareowner groups want current income. XYZ has been known for steady though modest growth over time.

Corporate customers used a lot of XYZ's product and were interested in how the product could be improved over time for a small incremental cost. Most families used only a small amount of XYZ's product, but that small amount was a critical ingredient for them, and there were no readily available substitutes. Thus, the stakes of the different customer

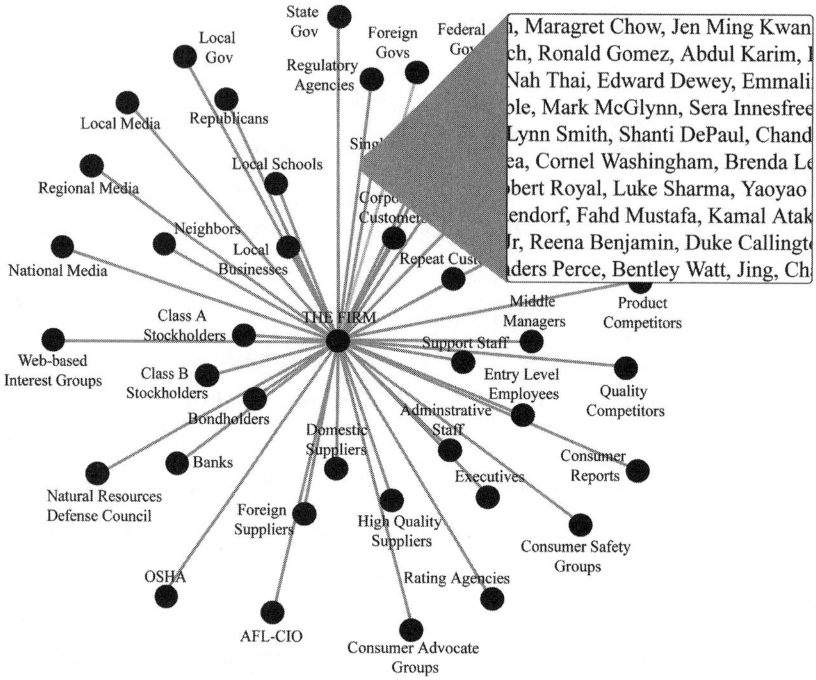
State Gov
Local Gov
Foreign Govs
Federal
Regulatory Agencies
Local Media
Republicans
Regional Media
Local Schools
Neighbors
Local Businesses
National Media
Repeat Cus
Class A Stockholders
THE FIRM
Middle Managers
Product Competitors
Support Staff
Web-based Interest Groups
Class B Stockholders
Entry Level Employees
Quality Competitors
Bondholders
Adminstrative Staff
Domestic Suppliers
Banks
Consumer Reports
Executives
Natural Resources Defense Council
Foreign Suppliers
High Quality Suppliers
Consumer Safety Groups
OSHA
Rating Agencies
AFL-CIO
Consumer Advocate Groups
Maragret Chow, Jen Ming Kwan
Ronald Gomez, Abdul Karim,
Nah Thai, Edward Dewey, Emmali
Mark McGlynn, Sera Innesfre
Lynn Smith, Shanti DePaul, Chand
Cornel Washingham, Brenda L
Royal, Luke Sharma, Yaoyao
Fahd Mustafa, Kamal Ata
Reena Benjamin, Duke Calling
Perce, Bentley Watt, Jing, Ch

3.3. Specific stakeholder map for XYZ Company

segment stakeholders differed. One consumer advocate group was concerned about the effects of XYZ's product decisions on the elderly, who were for the most part highly dependent on XYZ's products. Another consumer advocate group was worried about other XYZ products in terms of safety. By generalizing the marketing approach and applying it, the variety of stakes that make up XYZ's stakeholders becomes more apparent.

As our examples show, the construction of a stakeholder map for the business as a whole is not an easy task in terms of identifying specific groups and the stakes of each. The diagrams are enormously oversimplified, for they depict the stakeholders as static, whereas in reality they change over time, and their stakes change depending on the strategic issue under consideration. Similarly, the construction of an accurate

---

■ Box 3.2  Stakes of Key Stakeholders in XYZ

Corporate Customers
—High users of product

Employees
—Jobs and job security

Customers
—Pension benefits

Shareholders
—Growth and income
  balance
—Stock price stability

Democrats
—High users of special
  products

Families
—Low users of product, no
  substitute

Consumer Organization #1
—Effects of XYZ on Elderly

Consumer Organization #2
—Safety of XYZ products

Republicans
—High users of special
  products

---

portfolio is no easy task, as the problems with measuring market share have shown. The task becomes even harder when we consider several implications of these examples.

The first implication is that some stakeholders play multiple roles. We might call this a "stakeholder role set," or the set of roles which an individual or group may play as a stakeholder in an organization. For example, an employee may be a customer for XYZ's products, may belong to a union of XYZ, may be an owner of XYZ, may be a member of the Republican party, and may even be a member of a consumer advocate group. Many members of certain stakeholder groups are also members of other stakeholder groups, and *in the capacity of a stakeholder in an organization* they may have to balance (or not balance) conflicting and competing roles. Conflict within each person and among group members may result. The role set of a particular stakeholder may well generate different and conflicting expectations of corporate action. For certain organizations and stakeholder groups, a "stakeholder role set" analysis may be appropriate.

The second implication is the interconnection of stakeholder groups. ABC Company learned that one of its unions was also a large contributor to an adversarial consumer advocate group who was pressuring a key government agency to more closely regulate ABC. Networks of stakeholder groups easily emerge on a particular issue and endure over time. Coalitions of groups form to help or oppose a company on a particular issue. Also, some firms are quite adept at working indirectly, influencing Stakeholder A to influence Stakeholder B, to influence Stakeholder C.

The DEF Utility could not understand why a consumer advocate group was opposing it on a certain issue that had no economic effect on the group. One executive spoke to a consumer leader who told him that the only reason that the group was opposing DEF was because DEF had not informed them of the proposed rate change before the case was filed. In short, the consumer group perceived that they had a different stake than that perceived by the management of DEF. DEF managers naturally believed that as long as the proposed rate change was in the economic interest of the consumer group and its constituency, there would be no problem. The consumer group perceived things differently, that they had a vital role to play as influencer or kibbitzer.

Analyzing stakeholders in terms of the organization's perceptions of their stakes is not enough. When these perceptions are out of line with the perceptions of the stakeholders, all the brilliant strategic thinking in the world will not work. In short, people are complicated and complex. Reducing the causes of their behavior to pure economic interests is not very clever, and it just doesn't work very well. Ignoring their economic stake would be just as deadly. The stakeholder mindset asks that executives remember that stakeholders are human and complex before jumping to easy conclusions.

The congruence problem is a real one in most companies, for there are few organizational processes to check the assumptions that managers make every day about their stakeholders. The analysis proposed here in terms of stakeholder maps, stakes, and roles must be tempered by a thorough understanding of the workings of the organization through an analysis of its strategic and operational processes.

### Business Processes and Capabilities

Large, complex businesses have many processes for accomplishing the objectives they have with respect to stakeholder relationships. From routine applications of procedures and policies to the use of more sophisticated analytical tools, managers invent processes to accomplish routine tasks and to make complex tasks more routine.

An organization may have identified its stakeholders and stakes, but if it doesn't build into its standard operating procedures a concern with creating value for these stakeholders, then there will be trouble. The problem is that many organizational processes are oriented toward control—controlling the behavior of employees and even customers and suppliers. We prefer to reorient these processes toward capabilities. What does an organization have to know how to do in order to create value for its stakeholders? Defining capabilities makes the question of control a subsidiary one.

Capabilities begin and end with what outcomes the business is trying to create for its stakeholders. Figure 3.4 illustrates this idea. When the company has a clear idea of an outcome it wants to produce, such as "employees who are dedicated to learning," then it can work backward to the correct policy and processes to support the creation of that outcome. United Technologies has traditionally paid for almost any employee education efforts. Its capability is to create an educated and

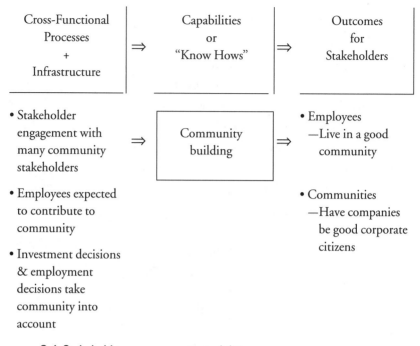

3.4. Stakeholder management capabilities

committed workforce, a necessity in the industries in which it operates. Its policies of supporting almost any educational effort chosen by employees produces an outcome of employees who are dedicated to learning, in part because they have chosen the learning themselves. United Technologies builds on this tradition by creating its own internal education programs as well, ensuring that employees understand that learning is a key component in business success.

Other stakeholder capabilities include building and supporting communities where employees live and work. The Dayton Hudson Corporation in Minneapolis has been engaged in this capability for many years, contributing to programs for lower-income families as well as the arts in Minnesota.

The strategic review process is another example of a good idea turned into "control thinking" rather than "stakeholder thinking." The idea behind this process is for the top executives in a corporation to periodically meet with division or strategic business unit (SBU) managers in a formal review session. Progress toward the planned goal is reviewed, and new strategies are sometimes formulated. Top executives are often accompanied by staff experts who have unearthed hard questions for the business manager to answer. These reviews are usually built into the strategic planning cycle and are used as methods of communicating expectations and evaluating both personal and business performance. The major problem with strategic reviews is that they become a game of "guess which number the CEO wants us to commit to." Strategic thinking can easily take a back seat to budgeting.

Strategic reviews need to focus on key stakeholder relationships and how they are changing. They need to focus on the capabilities that are being created to manage these relationships and continue the process of value creation. They must include a concern with governments, communities, and critics and be on the lookout for likely scenarios that may yield a quite different set of business conditions. The emphasis from the point of view of the divisional manager under review is to look good to the senior executives who are reviewing performance. The formality of most strategic review processes and the mixing of personal and business evaluation make it difficult for the division manager to pay attention to multiple stakeholder concerns, which may contradict established corporate wisdom about the factors for success in a particular business.

Most control processes are not oriented toward bad news. It is much easier to blame the stakeholder after the fact ("What senior executive in his right mind can hold a division manager accountable for a regulation that accounts for lost profits?") While responsibility for profits has been decentralized in most large multi-business firms, the responsibility for managing non-marketplace stakeholders (and some marketplace stakeholders) has not. Corporate public relations and public affairs are for the most part responsible for ensuring a stable business climate for all the corporation's businesses. Division managers naturally perceive that they have a lack of control over critical stakeholder variables. During one seminar on stakeholder analysis with division managers, the predominant comment was, "Great stuff, too bad my boss isn't here to hear it." After the same seminar to the top levels in the corporation, the predominant comment was, "Great stuff, too bad our people (the division managers) weren't here to hear it."

The stakeholder mindset must infuse all of a company's core processes and capabilities. By focusing on what outcomes are to be created for stakeholders, these processes and capabilities can keep the value creation proposition at the very center of the business. By constantly redesigning and monitoring these processes, and by engaging with stakeholders on a broad front, companies can keep these standard operating procedures and processes fresh and relevant.

### Everyday Transactions with Stakeholders

Transactions are where the rubber meets the road. They are where companies actually produce value for stakeholders. All of the mission statements, off-site meetings, process audits, and well-meaning managerial directives come to nothing if a company cannot produce transactions that create value. Most companies have many daily transactions with stakeholder groups. They sell products and services to customers, buy materials and services from suppliers, interact with employees, and engage in a number of community activities, from daily living to governing. Many of these transactions are fairly ordinary and unexciting, but in a company with a stakeholder mindset, there is always someone looking for a better, faster, cheaper way to produce even more value for stakeholders.

Transactions are connected to the mindsets of employees. When managers stick with a mindset of worrying only about shareholders, or worrying only about control, they simply leave out the value-creation possibilities with stakeholders. A stakeholder mindset builds into every transaction the possibility of creating value. It suggests that even with critics, there is value to be created and realized, but only through engagement.

The story of ABC is instructive here. ABC is an international company that has been built on a single brand with a large and devoted following. Many children grow up with this brand, and it leaves many pleasant memories. ABC prides itself on its commitment to children, and its corporate mission is explicit about the necessity of serving their needs. As sometimes happens, a number of adults continue to use ABC's products well into adulthood, and they have found multiple uses for ABC's products as well as new products. Some of these customers formed user groups on the Internet and began to contact ABC about new product ideas. ABC's response was to send a carefully worded letter from its legal counsel spelling out potential copyright and trademark violations if the user group persisted in creating new product ideas. The user groups thought that the company was not committed to its own products and was incredibly unresponsive to their enthusiasm. A group of managers at ABC finally discovered that this interaction with these customers was unproductive. It turned these user groups into focus groups and new product design teams, and they were incorporated into the thinking of the company.

By focusing on its internal procedures and processes, the transactions with these customers were unproductive and value was destroyed. By changing the mindset inside the company to one of voluntarily engaging with stakeholders, the transactions were radically changed, and new product ideas began to emerge.

The XAB Company is an interesting study in how a lack of consistency between a company's identification of stakeholders at the level of the business as a whole and its actual transactions with stakeholders can be dysfunctional. XAB understood its stakeholder map and had some organizational processes to formulate and implement strategies with primary and instrumental stakeholder groups. However, XAB sent some top executives, who had little understanding and no empathy with the causes of these groups, out to talk with several of these instrumental groups. As you might expect, the company made little progress with them. Perhaps the strategy and the processes are inappropriate given the objectives of the company. However, another interpretation is that the transactions between company and stakeholders have not given the strategy and processes a fair test.

Consumer complaints are another area where there is usually a noticeable breakdown in the transaction capability of a company. Many large corporations simply ignore consumer complaints and dismiss them as that 5 percent of the market which they would rather someone else serve. Not only are there few successful processes for dealing with consumer complaints, but the transactions involved are material for every stand-up comic who ever walked. Nothing is more frustrating to the consumer than being told, "Sorry, I wish I could help you, but it is company policy to do things this way." One consumer activist commented that being told it was company policy may well finish the incident for the manager, but it begins the incident for the consumer advocate. Several successful companies seem to "overspend" on handling consumer complaints. IBM's commitment to service, P&G's consumer complaint department, and Nordstrom's philosophy of taking merchandise back with no questions asked yield valuable lessons in understanding the nature of transactions with customers. These companies act as if consumer complaints yield an opportunity for understanding customer needs, which ultimately translates into a good bottom line and satisfied stakeholders.

Mindset matters. Transactions are the bottom line. If execution is a problem for Bob Collingwood, he probably should explore the mindset that yields the constant barrage of problems. Bob needs to get his team thinking about how to satisfy multiple stakeholders simultaneously. Stakeholder-facing organizations seek to produce value in all of their transactions with stakeholders. This is a simple idea, but one that requires some depth of thought. What is required is asking the question of what do we stand for, and how do we create value for each of our stakeholders. Strategic thinking needs to be transformed into stakeholder thinking and thinking about the enterprise as a whole. That is Bob Collingwood's challenge.

# 4

## Stakeholders, Purpose, and Values

As he prepared for his two-day strategy meeting, Bob Colling-wood thought back to the conversations he had had with his team and their consultants over the past few years. The consultants had helped them map out the industry, identifying the strategies of the key players and what they were doing to try to change the rules of the game. They went through a process of identifying key strengths and possible competitive advantages. They even adopted a strategic intent to "beat the number-one player." But something was missing. As Bob began to think about why he worked so hard, about what might inspire him and his team, he decided that maximizing shareholder value just didn't do the job. It didn't get him out of bed each morning. Bob realized that if it didn't do it for him, and he had stock options, it probably wasn't inspirational for his people. What could inspire Bob and his team? Could they have a conversation about how they made stakeholders better off? Could they build in time to talk about core purpose and what they stood for, and what they wanted the company to stand for? He knew it wouldn't be easy to turn their dreams and aspirations into a business model that creates value for stakeholders.

STRATEGIC THINKING

Many models of strategic thinking have been developed over the years. Indeed, there is a whole industry of strategy consultants just waiting to help executives sort through the messes that people like Bob Collingwood are in.

At the core of these many ideas about strategy lies the question of the purpose of a business. Defining core purpose helps to set the direction for a business and explain "why we are doing this." The definition serves to motivate and inspire employees, as well as attract those who share the purpose. It distinguishes the business from its competitors in the eyes of customers and suppliers, and it sends a strong signal to communities about what kind of citizen the company will be.

Some people argue that the only legitimate core purpose of a business is to maximize shareholder value; we believe that they are mistaken, for several reasons. First, maximizing shareholder value is not an intrinsic value. The whole idea, borrowed and corrupted from Adam Smith, is that if companies maximize shareholder value (under very special economic conditions) then the greatest good for society will be the result, and it is the greatest good for society (according to this view) that is most important and hence holds the intrinsic value. Second, we believe that the changing nature of business has made the managerial model with shareholders at the center highly questionable and inappropriate. Third, even if shareholder value is one legitimate purpose, we see no need for it to be the only one. It relies on a very specialized kind of corporate form—the publicly traded company. There are many ways to engage in business, incorporated and unincorporated, formal and informal. All of these value-creation activities have to deal with *stakeholders,* and shareholder value is just inappropriate for many of them. Finally, recent research by Jim Collins and Jerry Poras has suggested that one of the features of companies that are "built to last" is that they pay attention to questions of vision, values, and core purpose. While these companies might actually maximize shareholder value, it is notable that they don't try to do that. Merck tries to invent medicine to help people. 3M tries to be innovative. Wal-Mart is fanatical about everyday low prices. So purpose and its fellow travelers, vision and values, can be broader than shareholder value, as important an idea as that is. In the words of one CEO, even if you want to maximize value for shareholders, you still have to create value for stakeholders.

## Strategy and Strategic Thinking: The Old Story

One of the major contributions of the development of the discipline of strategic management has been that executives can examine where the firm is headed, what the nature of its businesses will be, and how changes in direction can be made. In the early days of strategic management, this examination of direction was made via long and involved processes that contained lots of steps and made nice flow charts resulting in binders of data—which were for the most part never used. Setting direction was seen as the front end of the yearly planning process, which ultimately ended in the development of operational goals via management by objectives for the coming year. Many executives still complain that the yearly budgeting processes in their companies are disconnected from anything strategic; these budgeting processes are holdovers from the complex strategic planning processes of the past.

Given the changes we have outlined earlier, it is clear that such an ordered, bureaucratic process, symbolized by strategic planning at General Electric in the 1970s, could not possibly cope with the nanosecond, on-demand environment of the twenty-first century. The fact that many large companies still have the vestigial limbs of such a process deep in the heart of their budgeting and financial systems should not deter us from looking for a better way. During the past twenty-five years, strategic management has evolved into a dynamic field of scholarship and action. However, there are still only two main approaches.

Traditionally, strategy consultants, management theorists, and the executives who listened to them pretended that strategy had little to do with purpose, values, and ethics. For the most part they saw strategic thinking as a way of understanding the external forces and pressures impacting on a business. By forecasting the environment or analyzing the industry, strategists could find good markets in which to compete, or niches of markets that were underserved. The paradigm of this approach was outlined in 1980 in Michael Porter's groundbreaking book *Competitive Strategy*. For the most part strategists saw strategic thinking from the "outside in": see which way the industry is going, and then align internal resources and competencies to fit those trends. The questions that such an approach asked were: (1) What is the nature of competition in the industry? (2) What is the bargaining power of customers and suppliers? (3) What substitutes are possible? (4) Are there likely new entrants? (5) What are the steps in the creation of economic value in the industry? (6) How does our company add value?

The main idea of strategic thinking in this approach is to understand these forces and to either defend against them or find a place to compete where there are few competitors. For instance, in an industry with the likely emergence of new entrants (perhaps profits are high, making the industry attractive), a company may defend its position by tying up most of the available suppliers into exclusive long-term contracts, making it difficult for new entrants to gain a foothold.

The impact of other stakeholders such as government, NGOs, critics, and even communities was thought to be unimportant. If it were important, it would have been seen through the forces that shape competitive strategy.

In 1994 C. K. Prahalad and Gary Hamel published another groundbreaking book, *Competing for the Future*. They looked at a set of companies like Canon, Honda, Charles Schwab, and CNN. They noticed that these companies, which seemed to have a great deal of competitive success, did things differently. They established a firm intention to do something, then they went about doing it. And what they tried to do was audacious. For instance, a relatively small company like Canon simply declared it would "beat Xerox." In short, these companies saw strategy from the inside out. They formulated an intention, called "strategic intent" by Hamel and Prahalad, then they "stretched and leveraged" the resources they had to go after fulfilling the intent. Hamel and Prahalad noticed that these companies never just allocated the resources necessary to fulfill the intent. They argued that executives needed to "stretch," acknowledge the gap between aspiration and resources to spur the organization to invent new ways to use the resources that they had.

The kinds of questions that such an approach asked were different. For instance, (1) What do we want to be? (2) What do we know how to do? (3) How do we create a "misfit" between our aspirations and our resources? (4) How do we leverage the capabilities and resources that we have to fulfill our aspirations? and (5) How do we set stretch targets that foster innovation and change?

While the first question about aspiration is implicitly a values question, the answers that Prahalad and Hamel found were not. Often they found strategic intent in terms of beating the other competitors, "being number one," or some other statement of competition. Stakeholders, values, and ethics, while implicit in this approach, actually played a very small role.

Both of these methods of thinking about strategy implicitly assume the managerial model with shareholders at the center. While this is explicit in the outside-in approach, it is also there in the inside-out approach. It is important to see that each of these approaches has an implicit appeal to values. Values most clearly appear in the outside-in approach in terms of external stakeholders whose needs are not being met by a business. Sometimes these stakeholders protest, boycott, or organize some action against the firm, or they may go to government to try and force regulation of the firm. Outside-in companies, by maniacally focusing on shareholders to the exclusion of other stakeholders and focusing on the external world to the exclusion of the aspirations of employees, mostly take a view that stakeholders are problems.

Alternatively, taking the inside-out approach more easily accommodates the role of values and purpose in strategic decision making. Inside-out is rooted in aspiration, in what we want to do. That is a question of values, even if we answer it in terms of maximizing shareholder value. The outside-in approach tells us that we have no choice but to maximize shareholder value, while the inside-out approach tells us that strategy is rooted in what we want to do, and how we want to do it. If the external world and our stakeholders don't agree, then we have to engage in a process of change with them. Focus on products and markets (outside in) and you fit into what already exists. Focus on aspiration, purpose, and values (inside out) and you will change the world.

What is needed is an approach that captures the best of both outside-in and inside-out. This approach should take into account the fact that the managerial model with shareholders in the center is no longer appropriate in the global business world of the twenty-first century. This new approach needs to recognize the centrality of a wide range of stakeholders, the importance of values and ethics, while connecting these ideas to the very core value proposition of a business. In the following section we want to outline such an approach, which we call "enterprise strategy," "enterprise values and ethics," or an "enterprise approach to business." All of these labels amount to the same thing, since we believe that it is not appropriate to separate business from ethics and values.

## ENTERPRISE STRATEGY

Enterprise strategy has four main components, which are interrelated: (1) purpose and values; (2) stakeholders and principles; (3) societal

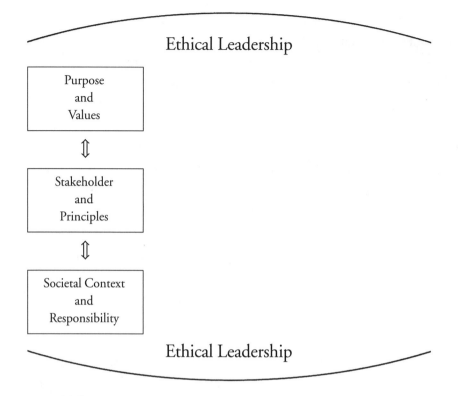

4.1. Enterprise strategy

context and responsibility; and (4) ethical leadership (see Fig. 4.1). We will outline the first three components in the following pages, saving a discussion of ethical leadership for Chapter 6.

### Enterprise Strategy: Purpose and Values

At many companies there are long complicated arguments about what counts as "mission" versus "vision" versus "values" versus "guiding philosophy" and the like. Each company must decide upon the right language for its unique culture and history. We want to suggest that the underlying issues are those of purpose and values. Fundamentally, these questions simply ask, Why? Why are we doing what we are doing? Why do we want to do that? or, sometimes, What do we stand for? A why-question is a request for a statement of the underlying values. These questions imply that we need to think more carefully about values, stakeholders, and what we want to leave behind.

Values come in all sorts of sizes and shapes, so a few distinctions can help us to clarify the kind of values with which enterprise strategy needs to be concerned. There are aesthetic values about what things are beautiful or what is good art. There are social values about what kinds of institutions are good and just. There are religious values about the worthiness of beliefs in a higher power. There are moral values about the goodness or rightness of certain kinds of actions that affect our fellow humans. There are values about all kinds of things, such as what makes an apple a good apple, or what makes a strategic plan a good strategic plan, or what makes a managerial decision a good one. It may help us to sort through this tangle if we distinguish two kinds of values, those which are intrinsic and those which are instrumental.

Intrinsic values are basic. Things that are intrinsically valuable are good in and of themselves. Intrinsic values are to be pursued for their own account and worth. Unless two intrinsic values conflict, we do not usually compromise on them. For many people, belief in a higher power is an intrinsic value. For some people, freedom to act however they see fit is an intrinsic value. For some, paintings by Picasso have intrinsic value. For some, being able to maximize their own or their family's happiness is an intrinsic value. Another way to put it is that intrinsic values represent the "bottom line" of life and its pursuits. Intrinsic values are the final answers we give to why-questions.

For example, if we ask you, "Why did you begin to read this book?" you might answer, "I want to be a more effective executive." If we ask you, "Why do want to be a more effective executive?" you might respond, "I want to get promoted." When we ask, "Why is that important?" you might respond, "So I can better provide for my family." At some point the why-questions must come to an end, and there we have reached an intrinsic value, something that you believe is good in itself, rather than as a means to another end.

Instrumental values are means to intrinsic values. We place instrumental value on those things that lead us toward the attainment of things, actions, or states of mind that are intrinsically valuable. Religious rituals or services that lead us toward our belief in a higher power may be of instrumental value. Constitutions that guarantee freedom of action have instrumental value to those who see freedom of action as intrinsically valuable. For some, the creative or artistic process has instrumental value insofar as it leads to the creation of works of art. For some, work itself has instrumental value insofar as it leads to the ability to maximize happiness or to self-fulfillment. These activities do not have value in and of themselves, but they do have value so far as they contribute to the achievement of intrinsic values.

Values are also about issues of character. When we try to teach our children values like respect, integrity, responsibility, and caring for others, we are trying to mold their behavior for many years to come in a variety of situations. These values are good in themselves, and they lead to good outcomes. Questions of character are about what kind of person we want to be. We need to take into account the consequences of our actions as well as how we want to live.

When we apply these distinctions to business, we find a set of questions that must be answered. There is no particular order to these questions, as they tend to go together. First, company values articulate a sense of what really counts in the company. ABC values dedication to customers, so in many decisions and conversations, invoking this value gives an answer to the question as to why ABC is embarking on a certain course of action. Values applied to business also serve to delineate what does not count. For instance, ABC's dedication to customers meant that they could not accept flaws in a billing system that made it difficult for customers to understand what they were paying for. Values empower action and they proscribe action. They serve as a kind of trump card to be invoked when there is some uncertainty about why a particular course of action is called for or absolutely forbidden.

A company's values evolve into a kind of "company character"—a statement of how we want to live and what we stand for. Sometimes company values appear to be divisible into business values, such as customer focus and teamwork, and ethical and moral values, such as respect and integrity. This distinction is artificial in a truly values-driven company, however. While customer focus clearly has implications for business, it is also about keeping promises to customers. Promise keeping is about morality and ethics, as well as business. Likewise, treating others with respect means delivering feedback, especially bad news, and can lead to very fast decision making. If a company is serious about its values, then each value has both business and ethical implications.

There is a myth that managing with values, and even thinking about values, is "soft and squishy." Nothing could be further from the truth. Think about the values conversations that you may have had with your children. They have a very sharp edge. If we are serious, then thinking about values is not about getting everyone to like each other, but it is about what is really important to us. This isn't easy, since values can conflict. Dedication to customers and going the extra mile for them can sometimes conflict with being innovative, or even being respectful. Standard company processes can fulfill one value while violating another. The answer is to have a conversation within a company about purpose and values that is truly alive, not laminated on a piece of paper in wallet cards.

Thinking about what we stand for naturally leads us to ask how we are serving each of our stakeholders. What value do we create for each of them, and why should they do business with us in the first place? Articulating such an answer to the basic value proposition is an important part of the enterprise approach. What we want to accomplish and how we want to act (our values) must be matched with stakeholder interests. Enterprise strategy must blend inside-out thinking with outside-in thinking. There are many ways to answer these questions. A company may focus on a single stakeholder or multiple stakeholders, or its values may be strong enough to delineate a field of stakeholders that have interests in these values. Later we will spell out these flavors of enterprise strategy.

Finally, we need to focus on what we leave behind. What kind of company do we want to leave to those who follow us? Much of the energy in today's business goes into trying to stay one step ahead of current pressures. How can executives like Bob Collingwood ever think about what they leave for those who come after them? Our view is that thinking about our legacy is a natural human desire. No one wants to be remembered as the executive that made a real mess that had to be cleaned up. We need to escape the picture of the disgraced CEO, forced out after two or three years for nonperformance. We can do this only if we think about the impact of our decisions on stakeholders over time. While the future is uncertain, our values are not. Managing by values allows us to define what we want to leave behind. And, personally, we need to think about the question asked by one CEO of a large multinational, "What do I do that can leave the business and organization better than I found it?"

There is much skepticism about values, stakeholders, and legacy questions in these times where business has lost the public trust, and rightfully so. If we are correct, the very business model that we use, the managerial view with shareholders at the center, makes it difficult to be anything but skeptical about purpose and values. Stakeholders don't count on this model, and issues of legacy go no further than the next quarter. Enron had a values statement that trumpeted "RICE," respect, integrity, communication, and excellence. These values were laminated in cards and there are videos of senior executives giving speeches about how important Enron's values are. It was all a sham. By all accounts,

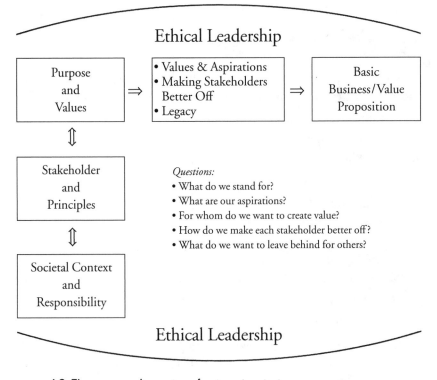

**4.2. The purpose dimension of enterprise strategy**

these values did not permeate everyday life at Enron. They seem to have been simply the result of a bad-faith effort to get stakeholders to believe that the company had their interests in mind, while executives were engaging in massive self-dealing. The fact that thinking about company values and purpose can be abused is not a reason not to think about them, but it is a reason that we should be cautious and skeptical.

Our view is more hopeful, but it is true that we have to be serious about these issues. Values are serious business. Employees can tell whether a senior management team is serious or not, and acting in bad faith destroys value for all stakeholders. Retailer XYZ has a clearly articulated set of values, and they routinely have conversations about safety in their stores. Executives at XYZ see safety as affecting customers, employees, communities, critics, as well as shareholders. Safety is a real value at XYZ, driving behavior, not something that is merely on a laminated card.

So, the purpose and values level of enterprise strategy asks an organization to articulate its basic intrinsic values, its reason for being, its inspiration for members. We can summarize this view by asking the following questions: (1) What do we stand for? (2) What are our aspirations? (3) For whom do we want to create value? (4) How do we make each of our stakeholders better off? and (5) What do we want to leave behind for others?

### Enterprise Strategy: Stakeholders and Principles

Wal-Mart answers the question of purpose through its slogan of "everyday low price." But even that slogan must have some intrinsic values and some aspiration behind it. Sam Walton's dream of making more goods and services affordable to the low-income and average consumer is still alive today at Wal-Mart. If this is to work at Wal-Mart, then the executives must be very clear about which stakeholders are most important (For whom do we want to create value?) and how these stakeholders are being served (How do we make each of our stakeholders better off?). At Wal-Mart, getting the products that customers want, when they want them, at great prices is clearly how the company makes customers better off. Less obviously, Wal-Mart's ability to deliver high-volume opportunities to its suppliers as well as work with them to establish state-of-the-art logistics and supply-chain management programs makes them better off as well. Traditionally, Wal-Mart offered great employment opportunities with the chance to buy stock and accumulate wealth. Indeed, a number of early employees who drove trucks at Wal-Mart became millionaires.

Having a clear purpose and the values that underlie it are not enough. You can think of answering the question of purpose as giving the logic for why stakeholders might do business with you in the first place. The second level of the enterprise approach is to give a reason for why stakeholders should continue to support your enterprise. Many companies articulate the answer to this approach in terms of how they want to govern their relationships with particular stakeholders.

Abbott Laboratories has an explicit policy of who their important stakeholders are. They realize that they can't solve all of their stakeholders' problems, but they strive "to balance multiple interests and obligations, and to be open to opportunities where [their] products, expertise and influence can help solve social problems and improve people's lives."[1] Their statement goes on to develop very explicit policies or sets of principles to deal with stakeholders like suppliers.

Abbott sees its suppliers as "an integral part of the overall success of Abbott Laboratories." Abbott wants its suppliers to commit jointly with them to complying with all relevant regulations and laws, fostering an environment of equal employment opportunity and working jointly toward "Abbott's commitment to global citizenship and making the world a better place."

In short, Abbott asks the following questions: (1) How are we going to manage and govern our relationships with stakeholders so that they will continue to be fruitful for both parties? (2) What principles and values are we committed to so that stakeholders can count on our support and our actions? (3) Are there principles and values that underlie all our stakeholder relationships?

Less well known is the case of Irwin Financial, which puts these ideas together in what they call a "guiding philosophy." At Irwin, their purpose is to "create superior value for all of their stakeholders, through a dedication to service, treating others as [they] would want to be treated, a long-term orientation, and the pursuit of the highest standards."[2] They are very explicit that the key stakeholders are customers, employees, shareholders, suppliers, communities, and society as a whole. All employees, from the chairman all the way down, are expected to

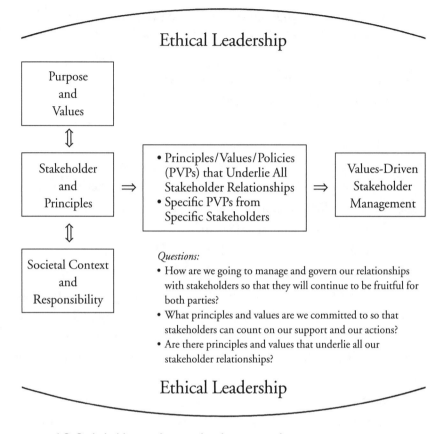

4.3. Stakeholders and principles dimension of enterprise strategy

know and live by this guiding philosophy in all that they do, from recruiting new hires to making everyday financial decisions for their customers.

### Enterprise Strategy: Societal Context and Responsibility

Being clear about and trying to realize these two levels of purpose (and values) and stakeholders (and principles), however, may not be enough in the highly charged global business environment of the twenty-first century. Some recent examples illustrate what is missing.

After being lauded for years as being on the cutting edge of management thinking, Wal-Mart has recently come under constant attack from critics. Its employment practices and its impact on communities have been called into question. Wal-Mart has been accused of underpaying its employees, not giving them benefits that they deserve, and discriminating against women. In addition, its practices with respect to suppliers (such as store cleaning services) and illegal immigrants, and its own practices (such as locking employees inside a store in some cases) have been severely criticized. In addition, critics have accused the company of having a dampening effect on surrounding commerce in communities where they locate, dominating traditional small-business owners as well as other chains, causing the "death of Main Street." A number of towns and localities have considered or passed "anti–big box laws" designed explicitly to keep Wal-Mart from locating in their communities.

Wal-Mart's initial response was to suggest that the millions of customers who shopped in its stores and the thousands of employees who were happy working at Wal-Mart validated their approach. More recently, the company has undertaken a more proactive response. It has redoubled its efforts on community issues, corporate responsibility, and environmental responsibility, and it has begun programs to make Wal-Mart stores friendlier places for women, both customers and employees.

In today's world companies must decide whether they are going in a direction that society appreciates and approves of, or not. Even if overall society approves of Wal-Mart, a substantial minority can have serious effects on the ability of the company to continue to create value for its stakeholders. Wal-Mart must put in place a program of "stakeholder responsibility" to be sure that it is in synch with the societal context or is actively managing any part of its operation that is out of synch.

The tobacco industry provides a good historical example of the necessity of such a program of stakeholder responsibility. Perhaps tobacco executives believe that "freedom to smoke" represents an important

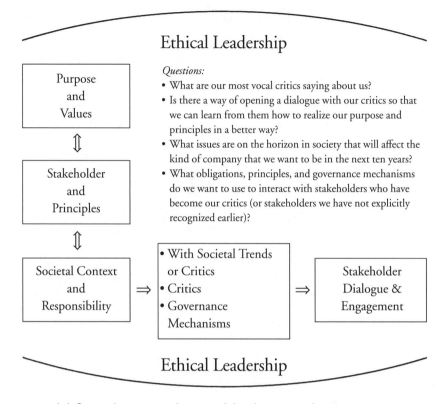

**4.4. Societal context and responsibility dimension of enterprise strategy**

liberty, and perhaps they have crafted a value proposition to make their stakeholders better off and articulated a set of principles by which those relationships will be managed and governed. They must also realize that the societal context has swung against them, however, and they must put responsibility programs in place to manage this context as well as possible. If the responsibility programs involve anything other than pure transparency and a real willingness to have dialogue with stakeholders, then they are likely to fail.

Stakeholder responsibility programs, like dialogue or engagement with stakeholders, that are not genuinely two-way communications will make matters worse. When the societal context is swinging against a company, it usually experiences a lack of credibility with its critics. Rebuilding this credibility is the first and most important step toward making enterprise strategy work at all three levels.

Questions to ask at this important societal context and responsibility level are: (1) What are our most vocal critics saying about us? (2) Is there a way of opening a dialogue with our critics so that we can learn from them how to realize our purpose and principles in a better way? (3) What issues are on the horizon in society that will affect the kind of company that we want to be in the next ten years? (4) What obligations, principles, and governance mechanisms do we want to use to interact with stakeholders who have become our critics (or stakeholders we have not explicitly recognized earlier)?

### THREE FLAVORS OF ENTERPRISE STRATEGY

There are many ways to put these pieces of analysis together into a statement of enterprise-level strategy. Purpose, stakeholders, and societal issues are all important ingredients and can be mixed together in a variety of proportions. In our experience, it is better to be explicit about these issues and to foster a real-time conversation about where the company is living its enterprise approach and where it falls short. We identify here three general types of enterprise strategies. Each of these strategies represents a whole set of particular responses and actions to the circumstances facing an individual firm. Hence, these generic strategies are broad descriptions of "what we stand for" and involve tradeoffs about the relative importance of stakeholder concerns, values, and social issues.

Briefly, these three types are: (1) a specific stakeholder approach; (2) a multi-stakeholder approach; and (3) a noble cause approach. We are certain that there are other approaches; this listing is meant only to stimulate you to think through the range of possibilities. We are convinced that there is more than one way to run a successful and ethical business in the twenty-first century and that new ways are being created every day.

### Specific Stakeholder Approach

One response to "what do we stand for?" is to concentrate the efforts of the company toward satisfying the needs of a small number of specific stakeholder groups, or the needs of one or two generic stakeholder groups. For example, if customer service and employee welfare are the basic values of a particular organization, and if everything the company does is aimed at achieving these intrinsic values, then in some realistic sense that firm stands for improving the welfare of customers and employees. Since these are but two of many stakeholders, this kind of enterprise strategy is dubbed specific stakeholder strategy. To adopt such a strategy is to try to maximize the benefits of the firm for a relatively narrow group of stakeholders.

P&G's statement of its enterprise approach focuses on consumers first, and if they do that well, they believe that their employees, communities, and shareholders will prosper. While a number of stakeholders are included in this statement, it is clear from both the actions of the company and its statement that it is consumers that are most important, and the key to its success. This may well be ironic given P&G's relationship as supplier to Wal-Mart.

Historically, companies in the computer business who align themselves almost totally with the customers and employees are good examples of how the specific stakeholder strategy works. Hewlett-Packard and IBM were almost legendary for their customer relationships and the way that they treated their employees. Creating value for customers and providing challenging and growth-oriented jobs for employees seemed to be ends in themselves for these companies. As the industry changed, however, the concentration on such a small group of stakeholders was problematic. The story of the rise of suppliers Microsoft and Intel to be the dominant architects in the industry is well known by now. While great customer and employee relationships are sometimes enough for success in an industry, those companies that rely on the specific stakeholder enterprise approach should take care to note that they are vulnerable to changes in other stakeholder relationships as well as changes in industry trends.

Thinking through the kinds of changes we outlined in Chapter 2, specific stakeholder strategies can be even more suspect against the backdrop of our old outdated friend, the managerial model with shareholders at the center, and its enterprise mantra of "maximize shareholder value." The main idea is that such an approach does not yield a very robust approach to thinking through how value gets created, and hence it is not a very good answer to basic question of purpose.

First, creating value for shareholders is rarely an intrinsic value. For it to become an intrinsic value, worth doing for its own sake, one must believe that there is an ethical obligation to act for shareholders in the same sense that one looks after one's own children. Even this obligation, however, doesn't yield maximum shareholder value. It's pretty standard ethics to believe that someone who acts in the interests of their children at the expense of others' children has done something wrong. So, at a minimum, maximizing shareholder value must include taking into account the effects of such action on others—that is, stakeholders. It is just too easy to rationalize acting in the interests of shareholders and ignoring the effects of these actions on others in the name of shareholder value. Even if you believe that shareholder value could somehow represent an intrinsic value, to actually realize this value, you must think about how value gets created for stakeholders. In short, you have to answer at least one of the basic purpose questions: How does our company make each stakeholder better off?

A closely related variant of the stockholder strategy might be called the financial stakeholder strategy. This version relies on satisfying the interests of the set of stakeholders who have financial stakes in the firm or who can heavily influence those stakeholders who have financial stakes. Thus, management actions are aimed toward stockholders, banks (both commercial and investment), other holders of debt, investment analysts, and so forth. The values of management in this case must dictate that financial stake counts for more than other kinds of interests. Management recognizes that ownership needs to be broadened to include any group who is risking its capital in the firm. The danger in such an approach was clearly stated by a friend of ours who is a professor of finance when he said, "You have to remember that finance is a report of the underlying activity, not the activity itself."

In effect, it is easy to use the stockholder or finance variation of the specific stakeholder enterprise strategy to mistakenly identify the report of the activity with the underlying activity. Business is about creating value for stakeholders. Almost every business affects its customers, suppliers, employees, financiers, and communities. If a strategy can be fashioned that makes some of these interests more important than others, it must also be on the lookout for changes in those other stakeholder relationships as well as societal change, and it must not mistake measuring the results from the "important" stakeholders for the underlying activity of the creation of value for all.

Sometimes a specific stakeholder approach is a good place to begin to ask the questions of enterprise strategy. When the new CEO of XYZ took over the company, it had been reeling from a series of badly integrated mergers and acquisitions. Executives from XYZ would introduce themselves by telling you what organization they used to work for. Everyone pressured the new CEO to "announce the new values" or "tell us what we stand for." He rightly refused. He always replied that regardless of what the organization decided to be, it had to offer great products and services to customers and be a great place for people to work. Until the organization could deliver on those values to that narrow range of stakeholders and achieve financial health by doing so, anything else was premature. Living a few widely shared values was more important than articulating a nice set of values that were not real.

### Multi-Stakeholder Approach

A second enterprise strategy looks more broadly at the stakeholders involved in the entire value creation process. Such an approach recognizes that it must take into account, at a minimum, customers, suppliers, employees, communities, and financiers. In doing so, many come to believe that by paying attention to this more complete set of stakeholders a company is engaged in improving the general quality of life in society. While there are many reasons for engaging in such an approach, it is consistent with such intrinsic values as improving society or Adam Smith's producing the greatest good for the greatest number of people in society.

For instance, the Unipart Group of companies, a large, privately owned logistics and automotive parts company in the United Kingdom, define their business philosophy as creating value for customers, employees, suppliers, shareholders, and communities, and they have a statement of principles that are important for each group. They claim that they have demonstrated the commercial success of this stakeholder philosophy for many years.

Some companies define stakeholders even more broadly. At Nokia, stakeholders are defined as "consumers and network operators, business associates and suppliers, employees, shareholders and investors, academia, the media, non-governmental organizations (NGOs), consumer associations, governments and authorities."

Whole Foods Markets is a prime example of this multi-stakeholder approach. They begin with a statement of the principles that serve as a foundation for the business, articulated as a "Declaration of Interdependence."[3] Whole Foods is explicit about how they want to treat customers, employees, communities, business associates, shareholders, and others. For instance, they state: "We view our trade partners as allies in serving our stakeholders. We treat them with respect, fairness and integrity and expect the same in return." Whole Foods sees their network of stakeholders as interdependent, hence the declaration. They claim, "There is a community of self interest among all of our stakeholders." They summarize their philosophy by saying, "Satisfying all of our stakeholders and achieving our standards is our goal. . . . One of the most important responsibilities of leadership is to make sure the interests, desires and needs of our various stakeholders are kept in balance. . . . Creating and nurturing this community of stakeholders is critical to the long-term success of our company."

## Noble Cause Approach

A third enterprise approach is to answer the question of the purpose of a company in terms that we might call a "noble cause." A noble cause is one that is worth signing up for on its own merit. Perhaps it is bringing affordable housing to more people, financing the dreams of ordinary citizens, making a first-rate education available to all sectors of society, or some other set of values that might be shared across an entire company. Noble cause enterprise approaches tend to inspire employees, but one has to be careful that such approaches are not just empty words.

One of the most famous cases in business history is the Merck's mission of "medicine for people not for profits." During at least part of Merck's recent history this led to the development and deployment of a tuberculosis vaccine in China (for a fraction of its costs), to the alleviation of terrible effects of river blindness for millions of people suffering in parts of Africa and Central and South America, and at the same time to a productive pipeline for more traditional drugs with robust and profitable markets. Whether Merck still has this commitment to its noble cause is open for question, given the controversy surrounding the drug Vioxx.

Stakeholders at Novo Nordisk

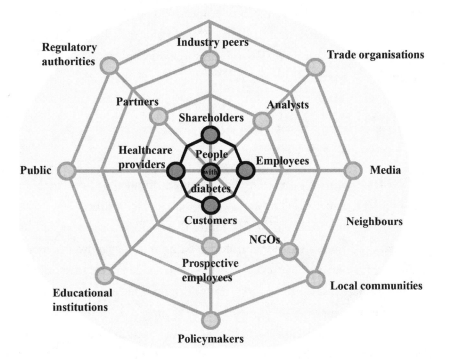

4.5. Novo Nordisk stakeholder map. The focus is on the inner circle with the person with diabetes at the center. Reprinted with permission.

More recently, Novo Nordisk has articulated its corporate purpose: "[We are striving] to be the world's leading diabetes care company, and each of us takes this vision personally. Our highest priority is the health and well being of people living with diabetes."[4] Novo Nordisk defines its stakeholders broadly as "any individual or group that may affect or may be affected by the company's activities." It pays special attention to employees, suppliers, customers, investors, public sector, and society. The stakeholder map of Novo Nordisk is instructive. Given their mission, they place patients in the center.

In each of these companies, and in the countless other companies that have such statements, a purpose is articulated that is worth signing up for. The purpose gives implicit (in many cases, explicit) recognition of the importance of key stakeholder groups. These companies usually engage in stakeholder responsibility programs or stakeholder dialogue and engagement programs to monitor the societal contexts of their actions.

### THE ENTERPRISE APPROACH AND CORPORATE SOCIAL RESPONSIBILITY

Many companies have applied our ideas about stakeholders to an area that has come to be known as "corporate social responsibility." And the growing importance of CSR around the world was summarized by one CEO: "Any multinational needs to be more transparent, open and fair. Over the next ten years CSR is the major issue for multinationals. They (we) have huge impacts on the world and we have to step up to it."

While we believe that responsibility is a core idea for an enterprise approach, we want to question whether or not the term "social" captures the essence of responsibility. Imagine that the CEO of Firm A is asked the following: "Well, I know that your company makes products that consumers like, and that those products make their lives better. And I know that suppliers want to do business with your company because they benefit from this business relationship. I also know that employees really want to work for your company and are satisfied with their remuneration and professional development. And, let's not forget that you're a good citizen in the communities where you are located; among other things, you pay taxes on the profits you make. You compete hard but fairly. You also make an attractive return on capital for shareholders and other financiers. However, are you socially responsible?"

We confess to having absolutely no idea what "socially responsible" could mean here. If a firm is doing all the things that Firm A does, then it deserves to be applauded and offered as an example for other firms, large and small, to emulate. If it is not doing them as satisfactorily as we think it ought to, then we could perhaps offer to help it do them better rather than appeal to actions and responsibilities that might lie outside the domain of its day-to-day activities. By talking of business and social responsibility as if they were two separate things, we might unintentionally be promoting the idea that they involve discrete thought processes and activities. In our opinion, the challenge is to promote a different way of doing business that integrates considerations of business, ethics, and society.

We believe that the enterprise approach is a better idea. Take your responsibilities to stakeholders seriously. If you define stakeholders too narrowly, be on the lookout for changes to signal that you need to broaden your definition. If you define stakeholders too broadly, be on the lookout for opportunities to focus your efforts. In both cases you are trying to create value for stakeholders. There is no need to think in terms of social responsibility. In fact, we might even redefine "CSR" as "corporate stakeholder responsibility" to symbolize that thinking about stakeholders is just thinking about the business and vice versa.

Having said that social responsibility isn't a necessary idea, let us hasten to add that it can be useful on at least two dimensions. The first is that it can serve as a way to monitor the societal context and responsibility level of the enterprise approach. It can focus some executives on looking more broadly at the business, and this is especially useful in a narrowly focused business. Second, it can serve as another way to take the idea of responsibility to community very seriously. In our experience, community is the stakeholder that is the most problematic, stemming from the shareholder ideology. Yet, by taking community concerns seriously, we can more easily see how our business creates value and how it could create value in a more effective and efficient way. Business gurus Stuart Hart and C. K. Prahalad have recently argued that there is a great deal of value to be created by looking intensively in communities at the "bottom of the pyramid," and global companies like Unilever have built thriving businesses on such a model.

## THE ENTERPRISE APPROACH AND THE ETHICS CONNECTION

Capitalism has a bad reputation. When we think about business we usually don't think about companies trying to add vitality to life, companies trying to alleviate suffering, or companies making their customers better off. In our experience, when we have explored noble cause approaches with executives the main problem has been with the executive mindset about business. We have had many conversations that went, "Well, that may be okay for a pharmaceutical company, but how do you translate it to banking (or electric power, or the grocery business)?"

The answer to this question is actually quite simple. You can finance people's dreams, provide power to make industries and individuals productive, and feed your communities. Skepticism comes from the underlying idea (no surprise to anyone who has read this far) that the business of business has nothing to do with creating value for stakeholders, serving stakeholders, or bringing about good in the world. It comes from the mindset that capitalism and business are necessary evils, driven by the profit motive. It is surely time to put this mindset behind us. Business in the twenty-first century cannot survive another hundred years of such thinking.

A hallmark of our approach has been to try to integrate a concern for ethics and values into the very nature of the value proposition of a business. In articulating its purpose a firm has to figure out who it will serve and how it makes each stakeholder better off. These questions are at once practical business questions and difficult ethical questions as well. It will not be very productive to separate these questions into "the business part" and "the ethics part."

Many companies simply don't go far enough when they articulate their ethics policies in terms of compliance with a set of regulations or a code of conduct, no matter how well stated or well meaning such policies are. In today's business environment every decision must at the same time enhance the value that gets created for stakeholders and do so in a way that can stand public scrutiny. An enterprise approach to business asks managers to put these two levels together. Today, it is business *and* ethics, not business *or* ethics, and certainly not "business ethics: a contradiction."

Bob Collingwood does not have an easy job. He can use enterprise strategy or an enterprise approach as a way to begin to build an answer to what his company stands for, an answer that will hopefully get Bob and his people to the office with a sense of inspiration. He can use it to put together business thinking with ethics and values thinking and begin to integrate the interests of all of his stakeholders. Talk is cheap. Part of the reluctance to commit to an enterprise approach in whatever flavor is that for it to be meaningful, you have to follow through in virtually everything that you do. Undertaking to lead a life with purpose is no small venture. Leading a company with purpose is even more difficult. The three levels of an enterprise approach must be embedded in a view of leadership we have come to call ethical leadership, signaling that we can't divorce the burden of leadership from its moral basis. (Chapter 6 explains this idea in more detail.) It is difficult to make all of our actions consistent with our values, and given that business is currently operating in an atmosphere of hyper-distrust by the public and other stakeholders, the difficulty of adopting an enterprise approach is magnified. We are still under the spell of the managerial view with shareholders at the center, and Bob and his colleagues must be willing to abandon that mindset if they are to truly create value for stakeholders. There are many ways to create value for one another. The beauty of capitalism is that it allows us to explore our dreams, do something together with our stakeholders that none of us could do alone, and create value for ourselves and those stakeholders. There is room for everyone in the organization to think of themselves as creating value for stakeholders. Chapter 5 explores some of the nitty-gritty details of understanding stakeholders and creating value for them.

# 5

## Everyday Strategies for Creating Value for Stakeholders

Let's suppose that Bob Collingwood, our beleaguered CEO, has followed our argument. He realizes that he and his team need a new framework that sees their relationships with a broad range of stakeholders as a matter of course, and that they see what they do in terms of managing for stakeholders. Further, he's already begun to think through his own enterprise approach but recognizes that this takes time to emerge from conversations, repositionings, new ideas, and just plain hard work. What Bob wants to know is, what are some concrete and practical techniques that can speed things along? How can he and his team begin to execute their daily decisions to more effectively create value for their stakeholders?

### SEVEN TECHNIQUES FOR CREATING VALUE

This chapter explains some very practical techniques that we have developed over the past twenty-five years working with companies around the world. These techniques are aimed at giving organizations an increased capability to manage for stakeholders. Just as the last chapter was aimed at understanding stakeholders and questions of purpose at the level of the firm as a whole, this chapter is focused on the process and transactional level. While these levels are informed by purpose and enterprise strategy, executives often work at these levels, especially when their organizations don't have a clear enterprise-level strategy.

We'll explain how to use these seven techniques to better manage your stakeholder relationships. The seven techniques are:

1. Stakeholder assessment
2. Stakeholder behavior analysis
3. Understanding stakeholders in more depth
4. Assessing stakeholder strategies
5. Developing specific strategies for stakeholders
6. Creating new modes of interaction with stakeholders
7. Developing integrative value creation strategies

Along the way we'll give you examples of how using these strategic thinking techniques has led executives to begin to exert more influence over their stakeholder relationships and helped them to create value for stakeholders.

### TECHNIQUE #1: STAKEHOLDER ASSESSMENT

Traditionally, both outside-in and inside-out strategic thinking have not paid much attention to systematically mapping the stakeholders in a firm to present a more comprehensive view. We noted in Chapter 4 that neither of these approaches is sufficient to take account of the business environment that most executives face today. They do not automatically account for, nor measure, the influence of multiple stakeholder effects on the firm. Both of these approaches to strategic thinking can be enriched to yield a better understanding of the firm's stakeholders.

One such process that has been developed is the stakeholder assessment.[1] You can think of a stakeholder assessment like a financial audit

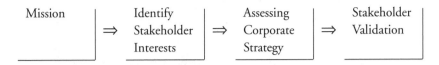

| Mission | | Identify Stakeholder Interests | | Assessing Corporate Strategy | | Stakeholder Validation |
|---------|---|-------------------------------|---|------------------------------|---|-------------------------|
| | $\Rightarrow$ | | $\Rightarrow$ | | $\Rightarrow$ | |

**5.1. Stakeholder assessment process**

that creates and certifies a financial roadmap for the firm. A financial audit is a report on the underlying activity that a firm engages in, not the activity itself. So, too, a stakeholder assessment reports on the underlying activities of the company and its impact on stakeholders. Especially in Europe, many firms have come to adopt what they call social reports as scorecards for how they are doing with their stakeholders. For reasons already covered, we prefer "stakeholder assessment" since it ties the relevant stakeholder relationships more directly to the basic value proposition of the company.

The stakeholder assessment process is consistent with the idea of mapping stakeholders (from Chapter 3) and enterprise strategy (from Chapter 4) but does not assume that a firm has a carefully articulated enterprise strategy, nor does it assume that a firm has a good idea of who its stakeholders actually are. Figure 5.1 depicts one such stakeholder assessment process consisting of four main tasks: (1) stating the corporate mission; (2) identifying stakeholder interests; (3) identifying corporate strategies for stakeholders; and (4) validation with stakeholders. This process can be tailor-made depending on the particular situation of a firm, and thus it should not be viewed as a rigid set of steps to be followed at all costs. Rather, Figure 5.1 is meant to serve as a conceptual guideline for managers who want to understand their environments in stakeholder terms.

*Task 1: Stating the corporate mission.* Many hours of executive time have been spent trying to formulate a statement of corporate purpose that is both meaningful and acceptable to a majority of the top executives in the firm. Often it is simply impossible for them to agree on a definition of the firm's business. Such conflict is good for the organization as long as it is productive and dealt with openly. The stakeholder assessment process begins when a provisional statement of the mission as it appears in the annual report has been articulated in the business press or has been explained to employees or to financial analysts.

Once mission and businesses have been identified, a generic stakeholder map can be drawn similar to those in Chapters 3. From the analysis of mission, business, and generic stakeholders a matrix can be constructed that shows the importance of each class of stakeholder to achieving success in each business. Assessments can be conducted at various levels. Perhaps a corporate-wide assessment is necessary, but almost any manager can conduct a stakeholder assessment that is relevant to his or her job. In some of these assessments at least a few stakeholders may well be inside the company.

*Task 2: Identifying stakeholder interests.* Once the generic stakeholder analysis has been completed, specific stakeholder groups for each business need to be identified. Here a specific stakeholder map for each business can be drawn, and a map similar to Figure 3.2 can be constructed. From the analysis of specific stakeholders, several versions of the stakes of each group can be deduced, again similar to Figure 3.3 and Box 3.2. The degree of detail should vary by the depth of understanding that managers have for stakeholders. The degree of detail need not be uniform for all stakeholders, with more effort spent on those groups that managers feel they understand relatively less well.

Once this initial analysis is completed a list of key concerns or issues must be developed for each stakeholder group. In many cases the information required to complete this step will be readily available from historical records and the experiences of individual managers. In some cases, however, the information must be systematically gathered by interviewing individual stakeholders, through briefing sessions with managers who are stakeholder experts or who are responsible for a particular stakeholder relationship, and by an analysis of the public

| Stake-<br>holders<br><br>Issues | Employees | Customers | Government | Community | Shareholders |
|---|---|---|---|---|---|
| Product Safety | 3 | 1 | 1 | 1 | 3 |
| Integrity of<br>Financial<br>Reporting | 1 | 3 | 1 | 3 | 1 |
| New Product<br>Services | 3 | 1 | 5 | 3 | 3 |
| Financial<br>Returns | 3 | 5 | 5 | 5 | 1 |

1 = Critical importance to stakeholder
3 = Somewhat important to stakeholder
5 = Not very important to stakeholder

5.2. Stakeholder issues matrix

record to determine positions of stakeholders on key issues. Again, this information can be aggregated at the corporate level and displayed in a matrix of stakeholders versus issues and concerns. Figure 5.2 is one example of how that matrix might look. Completion of a stakeholders/issues matrix enables the managers involved in the assessment process to orient themselves externally toward the issues and concerns of key groups. The managers can identify the sensitivity points in their external environment and pinpoint the issues or concerns that must be resolved if success in particular businesses can be achieved. The matrix also allows an aggregate look across businesses at the concerns of employees, consumer advocates, or local communities, enabling managers to think about the strategies which the firm as a whole may have with these stakeholder groups.

*Task 3: Assessing corporate strategies for stakeholders.* Tasks 1 and 2 create an external view of the firm by analyzing stakeholders and the key concerns of each. The purpose of Task 3 is to identify how the firm is currently meeting the needs of its stakeholders, that is, what the current strategy of the firm is with regard to each stakeholder or group of stakeholders. This strategy statement must include not only what the firm is currently doing with respect to a stakeholder but how the firm is accomplishing the strategy or the process of achievement, and what organizational unit within the firm has responsibility.

Identifying existing stakeholder strategies can normally be accomplished by a review process with the SBU, division, or functional managers responsible. In large and complex organizations, however, it may be the case that no one is responsible for a particular stakeholder group at the corporate level, with responsibility residing at the "strategy center" level. Corporate staff in public relations or public affairs may have functional responsibility for nontraditional stakeholder groups such as consumer advocates, the media, and government, and they may be formulating programs in virtual isolation from the strategy center managers. It will be difficult in such cases to articulate a strategy for the corporation as a whole toward a particular stakeholder or set of stakeholders. Also, the corporate strategy may well be inconsistent with the programs undertaken at the lower levels in the firm.

*Task 4: Validation with stakeholders.* The purpose of this step is to gather together the results from employee surveys, customer satisfaction polls and focus groups, feedback from industry analysts, and stakeholder dialogues with communities, NGOs, or other stakeholders. After identifying stakeholders, issues, and current strategies, executives can match these results against the data from stakeholders. One key set of questions to ask here is: How are we creating value for a stakeholder?

What is our assessment of how we are doing? What is the stakeholder's assessment? What needs to be changed?

For a company that already has a good understanding of its stakeholder picture and has consciously attempted to think through how it creates value for each stakeholder group, stakeholder assessments happen as a matter of execution. But even in those companies there may be one or two stakeholder groups who need more attention. If a company has an explicit specific stakeholder approach, then a stakeholder assessment on those who are not key stakeholders can be useful.

### TECHNIQUE #2: STAKEHOLDER BEHAVIOR ANALYSIS

At a concrete level, managers who interact with key stakeholders need to think through the range of stakeholder reactions and behaviors. Many have found it useful to think through a stakeholder's actual or current behavior, then to think through how changes in that behavior could help the company or, alternatively, how changes in stakeholder behavior could hurt the company. Segmenting stakeholder behavior (and potential behavior) into these three categories can lead to a more in-depth understanding of the value creation process. Let us be more specific.

The first, actual or observed behavior, asks the manager to set forth those behaviors that have been observed of a particular stakeholder. The set of actual behaviors describes the current state of the relationship between organization and stakeholder on the issue in question. It may even describe responses to existing strategic programs, where such programs are under way.

The second category of behavior, cooperative potential, asks the manager to list concrete behaviors that could be observed in the future that would help the organization achieve its objective on the issue in question. Or, what could a stakeholder group do to assist the business to realize its purpose? Cooperative potential sets forth the best of all possible worlds in terms of what a stakeholder could do to help. It is useful to look at cooperative potential as relative to actual behavior. Thus, *cooperative potential represents the changes in actual behavior that would be more helpful to the business.*

The third and final category of behavior, competitive threat, asks the manager to list those behaviors that could be observed in the future that would prevent or help to prevent the organization's achieving its goal. Competitive threat represents the worst of all possible worlds, and again it is useful to consider it as relative to actual behavior. By thinking through what a particular group could do to hurt an organization's chances of success, a manager can understand the downside risk associated with dealing with stakeholders.

By dividing the analysis of behavior into these three categories, the manager, in essence, thinks through the range of options that a particular stakeholder group has in terms of possible behaviors. Not all of the behaviors under cooperative potential and competitive threat will be observed in the future, nor will some of them be very likely. By adopting the schema of cooperative potential and competitive threat, the organization can undertake specific actions that seek to maximize cooperative potential or prevent (minimize) competitive threat.

For executives who deal with stakeholders every day and who have an intuitive sense of how a stakeholder can help and hurt the business, this technique adds nothing new. By focusing on behavior, it asks executives not to immediately jump to wondering if a stakeholder is for them or against them but to focus on the value creation process and ask what behavior must occur for effective value creation to take place. For many organizations that define their stakeholders very broadly to include groups that may be outside the day-to-day operations of the business, thinking through concrete behaviors can be a useful prelude to dialogue and engagement.

ABC Company had a stakeholder group that had been quite critical of the company's action over time. It did an analysis of actual behavior, cooperative potential, and competitive threat and decided that the best it could hope for was for the stakeholder to simply leave ABC alone. It could then determine what the stakeholder's real problem was with ABC's operations around customer service. ABC responded to these concerns, and the stakeholder simply stopped criticizing ABC. By focusing on concrete behaviors rather than getting the stakeholder to change its attitude, ABC was able to create value for the stakeholder and others as it had to spend little resources responding to the criticism.

### TECHNIQUE #3: UNDERSTANDING STAKEHOLDERS IN MORE DEPTH

Each of us sees the world from our own point of view—from a mindset that we have developed consciously and unconsciously over our entire lives. We make assumptions about the way the world works, about what makes a business successful, and about what makes other people tick. Sometimes we aren't even aware of those assumptions. Part of the main argument of this book is that some of those assumptions about why a business is successful are no longer appropriate. Whether you agree or not, the fact is that communicating with others who have different mindsets is a difficult, yet crucial task in today's business world.

It is easy to claim that a group we find difficult to communicate with is "irrational" or "acting on emotion," especially when there is a lot at stake. Critics of a business are often lumped together in such a category. We want to suggest something different. Whenever you are tempted to just throw up your hands and exclaim a stakeholder's irrationality or emotion, try substituting the phrase, "I just don't understand that stakeholder's point of view." It may be that a group's interests is different from those of a company or executive. It may be that the external forces and pressures on that group are hard to understand. Or, it may be that the group is motivated or inspired by a different set of values. Wouldn't it be nice to know? That way we could be much more effective at understanding, communicating, and maybe meeting that group's interests.

In our experience, asking a simple set of questions can help to foster such communication and understanding, and leads to more effective strategies. We have found the following set of questions very useful in our work with executives:

1. What are this stakeholder's main interests? How do we affect these interests? How are we affected by these interests?

2. Who are the groups and individuals who can affect this stakeholder? Who are the stakeholder's stakeholders? And what is the stake (interests) of each?

3. What does this group believe about us? What assumptions are they making? What assumptions do we make about them?

4. What are the natural coalitions that could occur? Where are there joint interests? What do we and the stakeholder have in common? What are the major points of conflict?

5. What might cause a stakeholder to engage in behavior that is more cooperative? More competitive?

There is no one "right" set of questions that works for all stakeholders under all circumstances, but these will give a good start. In essence, answering these questions is the same as constructing a "theory" about why stakeholders act the way that they do and how that behavior could change. Managers have to put themselves in the stakeholder's place and try to empathize with that stakeholder's position. They must try to feel what that stakeholder feels and see the world from that point of view. It isn't necessary to sympathize or express a genuine liking for a point of view, but to play the role of a particular group. By trying to play the role of a particular stakeholder the manager can more fully understand the reason for a stakeholder's behavior and thus construct an explanation of that behavior.

This process of understanding stakeholders in more depth is only as good as the knowledge and data that go into the thinking. XYZ developed a strategy based on the best thinking of its internal stakeholder experts. These "experts" were wrong on a number of assumptions, and when the strategy was executed, one key stakeholder responded quite differently than expected, undermining the entire value creation process, or at least changing it substantially. Testing this understanding with real stakeholders, whether customers or critics, is crucial.

ABC Company tried this process and designed a role-playing exercise to enable its executives to simulate stakeholder behavior in a controlled environment. The executives were divided into "stakeholder teams" and were provided with data, films, and sometimes real stakeholders to help them take on the role. A strategic issue of importance to the company was then simulated with the executives over an afternoon or a day. The insights that were generated were remarkable. By putting themselves in the shoes of the stakeholders, executives were able to see the effects of their actions on groups that had different mindsets. Over the course of several years, ABC put hundreds of managers through this process and generated a much-enhanced capability to create value for its stakeholders, from the introduction of new services, to the repositioning of other products and services, as well as the generation of rich political strategies for dealing with governments, NGOs, and other nontraditional stakeholder groups.

### TECHNIQUE #4: ASSESSING STAKEHOLDER STRATEGIES

We have found in our work with companies that it can sometimes be useful to try to categorize stakeholders by their strategic posture. By "strategic posture" we mean their capacity for change in order to influence the outcomes of a decision. For instance, let us suppose that a particular stakeholder is very influential on the outcome of a project but is also very cooperative, and if we lost their support the results would be disastrous. Contrast this posture with one where a group has a large negative influence on a project that really couldn't get any worse, but if we could turn them around it would be an enormous help to us.

By analyzing current behavior, cooperative potential, and competitive threat of each stakeholder we have a surrogate for the potential of a stakeholder to affect the ways that we create value (see Technique #2 above). Obviously, we want to treat those stakeholders who have high cooperative potential and low competitive threat differently from those groups who have low cooperative potential and high competitive threat. Thus, we might first want to rank stakeholders in terms of their relative cooperative potential. This is done by asking the question, "which groups could most help us achieve our objective?" or simply by classifying the groups by a simple scheme such as "high CP," "somewhat high CP," "somewhat low CP," and "low CP." The same can be done for competitive threat. (It is an enlightening exercise to go through a similar analysis as if we were our competitors. Competitors often have differing sets of stakeholders.) There are at least four categories of groups: (1) those groups with relatively high cooperative potential and relatively high competitive threat ("swing" stakeholders); (2) those groups with relatively low CP and high CT ("defensive" stakeholders); (3) groups with relatively high CP and relatively low CT ("offensive" stakeholders); and (4) groups with relatively low CP and CT ("hold" stakeholders). We would next check our classification and discount the CP and CT of groups that are not even remotely possible. That is, if a stakeholder group has high cooperative potential but we know from past experience that we cannot turn it around within the time frame of the strategic program we are developing, we must discount the CP of that group and perhaps cycle it to a higher level in the corporation. Through this exercise, we get a final picture such as that shown in Figure 5.3.

Swing stakeholders have a strong ability to influence the outcome of a particular situation. Hence, strategies that seek to change the rules by which the firm interacts with those stakeholders are appropriate. In general, new strategies are called for, and sometimes support programs are necessary to help.

Defensive stakeholders can be of relatively little help but can take steps

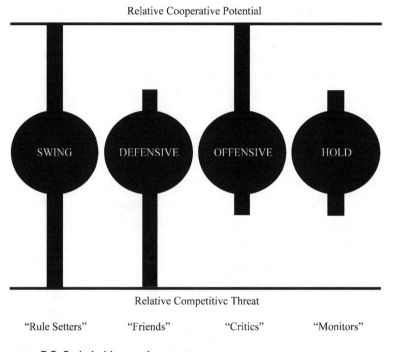

Relative Cooperative Potential

SWING     DEFENSIVE     OFFENSIVE     HOLD

Relative Competitive Threat

"Rule Setters"          "Friends"          "Critics"          "Monitors"

5.3. Stakeholders and strategic postures

(behaviors) to prevent the firm from achieving its objectives. Defensive stakeholders often have current or actual behavior that is quite helpful, and thus their possibilities for improvement and (in turn) high CP are quite limited. Defensive stakeholders illustrate the maxim that one is most vulnerable with one's friends rather than one's enemies.

Offensive stakeholders can help a great deal in achieving objectives but pose little relative threat. Perhaps they are already killing the company on this issue, and their actual behavior could not be any worse. If there is relatively little downside risk, virtually any strategic program is worth a try, and opportunities for gain should be exploited.

Hold stakeholders can be of relatively little extra help or harm. We must remember that they may currently be quite vital, however. CP and CT measure changes in behavior, since we are looking at how to formulate new strategic programs or programs that are supportive of current activity. With groups who are unlikely to move, existing strategic programs should be sufficient. Also, hold stakeholders may well contain a source of great value creation. They may well lack power simply because no company has been able to satisfy their needs, or we may not have been creative enough to identify their real cooperative or competitive behaviors. They should not be forgotten but treated as a resource to be better understood.

Many executives misunderstand the position of a company vis-à-vis its critics. They are often hesitant to meet with critics lest bad behavior results. But, if we are correct, there may be little downside risk to engaging with critics. XYZ Company had a number of public critics who questioned its right to exist. XYZ's CEO finally understood that it was better to engage these critics and let them at least be a part of the debate rather than simply let them continue to beat up on the company. He realized that the current strategy the company employed of dealing with the critics by not engaging them was simply not working. XYZ began a stakeholder dialogue process that slowly began to show progress. Of course this dialogue and engagement process could not be done in isolation, as the concerns with XYZ's products and services had to be addressed as well. Mollifying the critics would not work any better than ignoring them. Committing to such a stakeholder dialogue process was part of a larger change effort at XYZ.

### TECHNIQUE #5: DEVELOPING SPECIFIC STRATEGIES FOR STAKEHOLDERS

Sometimes just thinking about these generic postures is enough to formulate effective strategies for value creation. We can sometimes add another layer of detail to the strategic thinking process, however. We can consider how these generic postures can be put to work to formulate specific strategies for value creation. Each generic posture yields certain

■ Box 5.1 Specific Stakeholder Value-Creation Strategies

Change-the-Rules Strategies
1. Formal rules change through government.
2. Change the decision forum.
3. Change the kinds of decisions that are made.

Offensive Strategies
1. Change the beliefs about the firm.
2. Do something (anything) different.
3. Try to change the stakeholder's objectives.
4. Adopt the stakeholder's position.
5. Link the program to others that the stakeholder views more favorably.

Defensive Programs
1. Reinforce current beliefs about the firm ("preach to the choir").
2. Maintain existing programs.
3. Link issues to others that the stakeholders sees more favorably.

Holding Programs
1. Do nothing and monitor existing programs.
2. Reinforce current beliefs about the firm.

kinds of specific strategies that can then be tailor-made to individual stakeholder behavior given a particular business context. Box 5.1 provides a summary of kinds of specific value creation strategies that can be developed. In each case there is one additional option of focusing on how the day-to-day transactions with the stakeholder are executing. We shall examine this technique separately (Technique #6).

CREATING VALUE BY CHANGING THE RULES

The three strategies listed here are not mutually exclusive and can often be used in combination with each other. First, there are formal changes in rules, whereby the firm seeks to change the rules that have been enacted into law, evolved as administrative rules, or are perhaps even enacted in the charters of nongovernmental organizations. Value can easily be created by influencing the process of rule-making. A simple case would be getting specifications written into the rules that favor the needs of a company's customers, or a technology, or a capability that the company has.

Second, there can be a change in the decision forum, a change in who makes certain decisions and in where the decisions are made. In government, jurisdiction is an important issue and a strategic variable that should not be overlooked. The recent debacle in the telecom industry has largely been due to a changing and confusing regulatory picture where the technology doesn't obey the nice, clean regulatory guidelines that evolved over seventy-five years to regulate the industry. There have been winners, but also many losers, as the entrenched industry failed to create a forum for the decisions that might have allowed it to continue to be successful. There is no sadder case than the recent demise of the traditional AT&T, having now been taken over by its spin-off, the former Southwestern Bell.

Third, the firm can change the kinds of decisions that are made and thus refocus the relationship with a stakeholder around a different set of issues.

For example, several utilities have adopted a change-the-rules strategy with groups that have traditionally been interveners in their rate cases. One such strategy involves changing the decision forum from the adversarial rate case arena to surroundings more conducive to negotiation and communication, whereby the consumer leaders and the utility managers discuss upcoming rate proposals and try to agree on how to mutually proceed. Often the consumer group will still intervene in the rate case, but the company can gain an understanding of the consumer's point of view, and the consumer group does not feel bound to fight the company on every single issue. In fact there are some cases where the consumer group has agreed to certain company proposals, and both have agreed to disagree on others. By changing the forum in which at least some decisions are made, a company can begin to break down the adversarial barriers that exist between utility and intervener. Changing the forum of decisions also begins to change the process by which transactions are undertaken between company and activist.

Some environmental groups have successfully used a change-the-rules strategy with a number of industries by switching from the adversarial regulatory process to one of working with the companies on the inside to gain their support for environmental initiatives. One of the pioneers of this approach was the Environmental Defense Fund, which joined forces with McDonald's in their initiative to eliminate some of the waste that was generated by fast-food companies. Waste was reduced, generating value for McDonald's in terms of profits and value for environmentalists in terms of less waste in landfills.

### Creating Value with Offensive Strategies

A number of programs can be used to bring about cooperative potential with stakeholders. Stakeholders who have high cooperative potential may well have an adversarial relationship with the firm that is so bad that virtually any change will have a positive effect. Thus, there are a wide range of strategies that must be carefully analyzed to bring about cooperative potential. Included in this range of options are: (1) changing the stakeholder's beliefs about the firm; (2) doing something (anything) different; (3) trying to change a stakeholder's objectives; (4) adopting the stakeholder's position; and (5) linking the issue to others that the stakeholder sees more favorably.

There are numerous examples of these types of strategies. The simplest type of strategy to change a stakeholder's beliefs about the firm is a product or service repositioning program. New uses are found for old products, which change the customer's ideas about the product or service. By trying to change a stakeholder's beliefs about the firm, managers are betting on the fact that the stakeholder's behavior is a result of erroneous assumptions about the firm. One company undertook a similar strategy by learning to listen to its critics, desiring to show the critics that the firm was made up of reasonable individuals who in fact were quite concerned about a particular social issue but who had little idea how to solve it.

If a situation with a stakeholder group is already quite negative, and if there is little that group can do to hurt the company further, then virtually any action is worth a try. However, random action or action that reinforces current negative beliefs about the firm can entrench and intensify the current negative behavior. The tobacco industry in the United States is a good example here. After being sued and settling out of court with the U.S. attorneys general, several firms undertook new strategies to open up dialogue with critics, promising more transparency than historically was true. Others simply changed their point of view and began to advocate for federal regulation and control.

A strategy that is more difficult than the two already mentioned is to try and change the stakeholder group's objectives—that is, to convince that group to want the same things as the firm. Many dollars are spent implementing programs aimed at changing stakeholders' objectives. Advocacy advertising campaigns are sometimes aimed at changing groups' objectives with respect to the proper role of government. Campaigns often trumpet the virtues of free enterprise and ridicule the efforts of government to interfere in market processes. These strategies should be used with caution as a net result can often be to change a stakeholder group's beliefs about the firm doing the advertising; namely, the stakeholder can come to believe that the ads are self-serving and a waste of resources. Little value may actually be created here, though executives and board members may feel better by fighting back.

On the other end of the perspective is a strategy to adopt the objectives of a stakeholder on a particular issue. This is standard operating procedure in the marketplace, or at least it should be, and can be carried over to other arenas as well. Labor-management cooperation can be fostered if union goals are accepted by management, and unionization can even be prevented in cases where management understands and adopts the goals of employees. Such a strategy is usually undertaken only after a long strike when both company and union are hurting. Of course there may be inefficiencies to such an approach, but if cooperative potential of a particular stakeholder is truly vital to the survival of the firm, then giving in has to be considered. One effective strategy is to link the issue under consideration to broader concerns of a particular stakeholder group, and to show that stakeholder group that its support on the issue is consistent with its support on a larger issue.

## Creating Value with Defensive Strategies

Defensive strategies are necessary when a stakeholder group holds the keys to failure on a project but cannot really help achieve its success. A typical situation that calls for defensive strategies is a trade organization's executives dealing with its membership. Quite naturally, organizations that belong to trade organizations can veto certain courses of action, and if they do not support the actions of the trade organization's management then the organization is doomed. However, there is little cooperative potential because usually the member organizations are as supportive as possible. Hence, the rational trade organization manager has to guard against loss of support from his or her members. The general question is how to prevent the degeneration of actual behavior into competitive threat.

Managers may not necessarily try to change the attitudes of the stakeholder but rather may try to reinforce current attitudes. In a sense the manager must "preach to the choir" who are already believers. By constantly reinforcing current beliefs the manager protects against changes in beliefs that would yield more negative behavior. Again, trade organizations are instructive, as are professional organizations. Annual meetings are replete with discussions on "how much the organization has done for you during the past year."

Stockholders are another case in point, for while there is little cooperative potential for stockholders as a group, there is relatively high competitive threat. If a great number of them try to sell the stock at the same time, value will be destroyed, not created. Hence we see the now-familiar ritual of the annual meeting, the annual report, and the road show for analysts.

## Creating Value through Holding Strategies

Even though some stakeholders have relatively little cooperative potential or competitive threat, they may still be important. Strategies need to be thought through that maintain current behavior and that try to better understand the needs of these stakeholders. Holding stakeholders can be sources of innovation simply because we have not thought through how these stakeholders could really help or hurt the company. There is latent value in these stakeholders.

### TECHNIQUE #6: CREATING NEW MODES OF INTERACTION WITH STAKEHOLDERS

The transactional level of analysis is the bottom line of managing for stakeholders. It is where there is a concrete interaction between the company and its key stakeholders. More recently this has gone under the rubric of "strategy execution," the carrying out of strategic tasks and seeing them through to completion. Obviously, we change the value creation process with stakeholders when we change the way that the company interacts on an ongoing and daily basis with its stakeholders, from customers to communities.

In our years of experience with global companies we have observed at least four typical ways that companies interact with their stakeholders. We have called these approaches *ignore the stakeholders; the public relations approach; implicit negotiations;* and *engagement, dialogue, and negotiation.*

### Ignore the Stakeholders

Trivial as it may sound, some organizations simply do not interact with those groups and individuals who can affect or who are affected by them. Perhaps such inaction is a form of denial, or perhaps it is simply a breakdown of organizational processes such as environmental scanning, which, after all, are not infallible. Or perhaps ignoring certain stakeholder groups is a result of using the managerial model in a world where it is no longer appropriate. Regardless of the underlying reasons, organizations that ignore their stakeholders are in for big trouble, sooner or later.

Company KSD found that they ignored a particular stakeholder group that knew how to use the political process to affect KSD. The group got a state legislature to sponsor a bill that would affect KSD's operations in the state. By the time that KSD managers organized to try to defeat the bill, it already had enough sponsors to pass. KSD had to forego a large sum of potential profits in that state because of the restrictive legislation.

Many companies have made this mistake in their conversations with communities. They will acknowledge the importance of customers, employees, suppliers, and financiers but ignore the communities and sometimes critics, or they may engage in a halfhearted and nonstrategic attempt at philanthropy. In a relatively free and open society, companies do this at their own peril. Community leaders, critics, and even disaffected employees can use the legal and political process as a way to "transact business" with the company—often at the expense of the value creation process.

The most glaring historical example was the petroleum industry and the rise of OPEC, which the industry ignored for many years. When OPEC was initially formed in 1960 it was a weak signal to oil company planners. In the words of one executive, "We knew OPEC was around, we thought it was some kind of joke."

When inaction occurs between a company and a stakeholder, then the stakeholder can take its needs to another firm to be satisfied or it will begin to use its political power to try to force a response from the firm. Once the initial use of coercive power is made, the conflict can escalate, and the firm must play "catch up." We see this dynamic now being played out with Wal-Mart's relationship with its critics and with communities where it would like to locate.

A variant of the "ignore the stakeholder" strategy occurs when no resources are allocated to deal with a stakeholder or with possible future stakeholders. The firm may as well be ignoring the stakeholder, for the absence of resources sends the same signals. The lack of any organized effort means that the firm will not participate in the initial phase of issue identification, where it is crucial to influence the discussion and the definition of the issue.

One obvious way for organizations to interact with stakeholders more effectively is simply not to ignore them. Some organizational process or some manager must be responsible for continually surfacing the transactions that are, and are not, made with the organization's stakeholders.

## The Public Relations Approach

Most large organizations have public relations departments whose task is to communicate with the public. Many businesses depend heavily on the PR department to interact with stakeholders such as communities or critics. Most PR people are trained as communications experts in schools of journalism. Typical stakeholder interactions revolve around communications programs, where the PR people tell the stakeholders or "publics" (or worse still, "audiences") about the company's plans and how the plans affect the stakeholder. Often this approach simply incites a stakeholder group to action.

Alternatively, PR people undertake speaker programs and community leader luncheons, whereby so-called opinion leaders are informed as to the company's plans. The common thread of the PR approach is that any communication is one-way. PR people tell our story, sometimes with the help of PR consulting firms who put together catchy campaigns to please executives. The focus of such campaigns is image, and while the image of the firm is not to be overlooked it does not automatically follow that a firm with a good image is very well off in terms of meeting stakeholder needs.

Public relations is a vital part of the business mix, but it needs to be integrated into the strategic thinking process of the firm. It is no longer practical to separate the public relations part of a decision from the business part. Both have to be integrated into the basic value proposition of the business. Thus, how we communicate and interact with our key stakeholders, from customers to investors and communities, is fair game for division managers, CEOS, and PR executives.

### Implicit Negotiation

A third method of interaction is for the firm to take stakeholder concerns into account in the formulation of value creation strategies. Because the firm has tried to take stakeholder concerns into account before a strategy was implemented, it can often mitigate any objections that a group may have. Many companies we are familiar with try to anticipate stakeholder interests in products, services, and initiatives.

The problem with implicit negotiation is that it is only as good as the attribution of positions to stakeholders that goes on in the planning stages. If implicit negotiation is to be effective there must be a conscious decision to rely on secondary data rather than asking the stakeholders themselves. The need to validate information necessary for implicit negotiation leads naturally to a more direct process of engagement with stakeholders' explicit negotiation.

### Engagement, Dialogue, and Negotiation

In our experience the companies that are the best at creating value for stakeholders are actively engaged with those stakeholders. They have managed to create a conversation, multiple channels of communication, and explicit dialogues with key stakeholder groups that are continuous.

In these companies, communication processes with stakeholders are two-way. If managers cannot understand stakeholders' positions and if stakeholders cannot understand the positions of the firm, then each must find a way to overcome such a barrier. Communication is quite complicated. Each party brings a set of biases, and the possibilities for misunderstanding are numerous. The further apart an organization is from its stakeholders in terms of shared values, the harder truly two-way communication will be.

The key to successful communication is perhaps the credibility of the communicating parties, and credibility is "party-relative." While many companies have credible relationships with their stakeholders, building such relationships can be a painful, time-consuming, and expensive process. Nike's process of establishing stakeholder dialogue is very instructive.

Nike was accused by critics of fostering child labor and unsafe working conditions. Nike owns no factories, but it does have supplier relationships with factories all over the world, especially in East Asia. Nike undertook an original investigation led by former U.N. Ambassador

Andrew Young. The report uncovered some problems that Nike tried to fix. This did not satisfy the critics, and eventually Nike undertook an extensive revamping of its relationship with its suppliers. It articulated principles that it expected suppliers to adhere to and put in place a strict system of inspection and penalties. Nike also undertook an explicit program of stakeholder dialogue and stakeholder engagement to be sure that it understood its critics. While it cannot meet all of their demands, Nike is better able to compete in today's fishbowl environment because it has access to its stakeholders and what they believe about Nike.

When the Environmental Defense Fund and McDonald's sat down to formalize their arrangement for the waste project we mentioned earlier, participants recounted that there was a lot of effort spent on the details of the contractual arrangement and who had rights and duties. As the project unfolded, working together led to more informal negotiations. Where there was a set of formal rules by which all parties had agreed to abide, once some trust was established, the informal process was both more efficient and effective.

The advantages of informal negotiations are obvious. There are no restrictions on communications, and positions do not have to be taken "for the record." Formal proceedings are not conducive to creative solutions, and experimentation is not encouraged. When methods of informal negotiation are used to their fullest, the formal proceedings, or contracts, if they exist, can become ritualistic and virtually unnecessary. "Formality" is a relative term. A simple meeting with a stakeholder group with whom the company has had no previous contact can be a formal proceeding, while meetings among groups with long-standing relationships can be informal. Effective transaction processes make use of informal negotiations.

A related issue is where negotiations take place and what the setting is for the talks. One consumer leader ran a joint panel for members of industry and consumer leaders at a resort to remove both groups from the day-to-day battles and to foster real communication. Another activist complained that business leaders do not understand that most of the members of his group are volunteers and hence cannot come to daytime meetings simply because they all have jobs. He appreciates the well-meaning managers who try to involve group members in corporate decisions, but the setting is all wrong. Setting and turf can be intimidating if used incorrectly, and they can be destructive of meaningful stakeholder engagement. They are variables that must be thought through when planning explicit negotiations with stakeholder groups.

One interpretation of our idea of stakeholder engagement is that managers need to understand and communicate with stakeholders that they should communicate for the sake of communication. Unfortunately, this has become a ritualized process in some companies through their commitment to issuing "social reports" that are often reports on the dialogues that a company has with stakeholders (usually not defined in terms of customers and suppliers). Communication is not an end in itself but a crucial task to the process of value creation. Actions demand that managers be prepared to make proposals, to respond to proposals from stakeholder groups, and to be willing to compromise. Managers who are not experienced "traders" will often experience difficulty in their stakeholder transactions, just as they will experience difficulty in their dealings with their peers.

Company XAC tailor-made a stakeholder process to surface "bargaining chips," those positions on issues on which the company can compromise. The process forced managers who interact with stakeholders to explicitly recognize where the interests of the company and key stakeholders overlapped. These managers went to stakeholders with a careful understanding of what they needed to give up to get stakeholder support or action on an issue. The process was not infallible, but it did force those managers to think about exchange and compromise as the primary media of transaction. There are times when managers must take risks and commit themselves to positions that run counter to company policy. If managers are not willing to do so, then real negotiation cannot take place because the limits of the transaction can never be reached.

One favorite method of interacting with stakeholders deserves careful scrutiny; namely, the use of unilateral action. Unilateral action involves taking actions alone, without any communication beforehand. Companies that ignore their stakeholders perform unilateral action, but many who communicate regularly and negotiate with their stakeholders do so as well. The paradigm of unilateral action comes to us from foreign policy: "We'll put the missiles in Cuba and see what Kennedy does," or "We'll take the hostages in Iran and see how Carter responds," or "We'll announce that we have a nuclear program and see how leaders in China, Japan, South Korea, and the United States respond."

In each case an action is taken and a response is provoked. Unilateral action increases the risk of conflict escalation. Each side has a tendency to overreact, because it is not certain "where the other is coming from." A company's assumptions about the stakeholder are put to the test. Companies that unilaterally announce a plant closing escalate any possible conflict with their employees at the plant that is affected and at all other plants as well. Internally, managers who take unilateral actions with respect to their subordinates are feared and often undermined. Bad news is not easy to tell, and conflict is difficult to manage, but the use of unilateral action makes it worse. The conflict or bad news will not go away, and we will be called to account for the unilateral action itself.

The key to successful transactions with stakeholders is for managers to think in terms of "win-win" solutions—how the many parties that are affected by a particular program can come out as winners. There are few situations in the real world where there are only winners and losers. Even in strictly competitive markets, one must realize that if the game is truly won and major competition is eliminated, there is no more fun to be had and an antitrust suit to be fought. Where there is conflict, interests are partially opposed, but because there is a conflict of some interests among parties, it does not follow that there is a total and complete conflict of interest. It does not pay to lose sight of those areas where interests coincide. Managers responsible for interactions with stakeholders must constantly think in terms of how the other party can win. What are the currencies in which the stakeholder is paid? Perhaps it is exposure or media attention, or maybe it is in forcing the company to change. Can we give something in terms of these currencies? If so, the chances for successful transactions are increased. The stakeholder theories developed in formulating strategic programs are invaluable in trying to formulate proposals and responses that are mutually satisfying. The natural bias of managers to translate their own payoffs, usually in terms of economics, to stakeholders, must be avoided.

### TECHNIQUE #7: DEVELOPING INTEGRATIVE STRATEGIES FOR STAKEHOLDERS

Even though there are programs for individual stakeholders, the sum of these programs may not add up to the desired direction for the company. Much value can get created by finding ways to satisfy multiple stakeholders simultaneously. Ultimately, stakeholder interests are joint and must be guided and coached into roughly the same direction. What is good for consumers needs to be good for suppliers, communities, employees, and financiers.

There are two basic ways to tackle this issue. First, we can recognize that there are commonalities in behaviors, interests, and the strategies that we have developed for individual stakeholder groups, and hence return to some of the techniques in the earlier sections of this chapter. Alternatively, we can return to our answers to the questions of purpose and values and try to find commonalities that appeal to multiple stakeholders simultaneously. Obviously, if your company hasn't made much progress on the enterprise approach, then the first method will be most useful to you. If you're well on the way to articulating what you stand for as well as values and principles, then the second approach will work.

Company XYZ is a consumer products business relying on multiple brands and products for its success. It uses a full range of chemistry in the development of these products but is heavily regulated. It had to decide whether to buy a smaller company in the industry but was unsure of the effects of the merger on a number of stakeholder groups. XYZ had a clearly articulated enterprise approach that involved paying attention to the safe use of its products. They discovered that some of the products of the acquisition candidate, while perfectly legal, were questionable from a customer safety perspective. By applying its well-thought-out enterprise approach, XYZ decided to forego the acquisition.

Merck's development of Mectizan to treat river blindness is another example of a strategy that satisfied multiple stakeholders simultaneously. Even though the people who suffered from the disease had no money, Merck decided to give the drug away, and in the words of one former executive, "Happiness broke out in the research labs." By seeing the interests of this "customer" segment as a joint interest with its employees, Merck was able to create value for the future.

The Grameen Bank in Bangladesh is known as a pioneer in the concept of microfinance, lending money to poor people so they can finance their small businesses and eventually become self-sustaining. The company understood its customers and their stakeholders well, and figured out that they could benefit by being able to communicate more easily. They began a telecom subsidiary that financed cell phones to key customers, who in turn would rent the phone to others so that market trips, prices, and supplies could be coordinated. By understanding a stakeholder's real behavior and by understanding the daily life of that stakeholder (and in turn that stakeholder's stakeholders) the Grameen Bank was able to create a business that at once created value for its customers, communities, and other stakeholders.

The purpose of this chapter has been to help executives like Bob Collingwood manage for stakeholders more effectively while at the same time continuing to work on the company's overall purpose and values. Obviously, the more explicit a company's enterprise approach, the easier it is to apply some of the techniques in this chapter. Let us caution you, however, that one of the most important parts of our approach remains to be discussed: ethical leadership. Managing for stakeholders is not for everyone and for every company. It entails a commitment to putting ethics at the very center of business decision making, and for the executive, this means that ethics and leadership have to go together.

# 6

## Leadership and Managing for Stakeholders

Bob Collingwood slowly opened the packet of information to discover columns of numbers and paragraphs of advice. It was his basic data for a yearly 360-feedback process that the corporate human resources group had mandated. The basic idea was for Bob and other executives to get input on their leadership styles and abilities, and the feedback was supposed to be anonymous so people could tell the truth. Bob spent the first twenty minutes analyzing the data, trying to figure out who had said what, even though he knew this was unproductive. The feedback, overall, was quite good. Bob was seen as a supportive manager who trusted his team. Almost everyone felt good working for Bob. But everyone also complained of how demanding Bob was, and how he didn't tolerate mistakes very well. A few mentioned that the group never seemed to get out in front of things, that they were always trying to catch up to what was going on in the world. However, the piece of data that stung Bob the most was the revelation that his team did not think that he wanted them to push back when they thought he was wrong. There was less transparency and openness than Bob thought he had. The feedback suggested that this was due to the tremendous stresses of the business. But Bob knew that he had to do something. Without openness and honest communication, he was sure that company politics and infighting would surely begin to creep in. Performance would suffer and it would not be fun to go to work.

As he reflected on the work his team had done on identifying its enterprise approach, its values, purpose, and stakeholders, Bob began to wonder about the implications of taking a stakeholder mindset to leadership. Wouldn't such a mindset put ethics and values into the very center of thinking about the role of the leader? Yet this was far from what he had read in the business best sellers and even heard in the leadership seminar he had recently attended. He knew he had to have a new vision about his role as leader.

## LEADERSHIP: THE STANDARD STORY

In the history of business and management, no concept has provoked more articles, books, heated conversations, and general buzz than has "leadership." Every bookstore is filled with volumes proclaiming "Leadership Lessons from X" where X is a famous historical figure, a sports coach, religious figure, or political leader. Even fictional characters are getting into the act, with books on leadership lessons from characters on *Star Trek*. There are long academic debates about the characteristics of leaders, whether leadership can be taught or is innate, as well as the proper role of leadership training in the business curriculum. Business executives are not immune. There are literally thousands of leadership seminars. Executives are promoted on their leadership ability or leadership potential. Many have marched to the clarion call of leadership guru Warren Bennis's pronouncement that "American business is over-managed and under-led."

Despite all the talk about it, there is little agreement on the basics of leadership, and there are few theories and models of leadership that can even be seen as competing. To understand this vast amount of writing on leadership and to adapt it to a world of managing for stakeholders we have to look at a number of issues:

1. The leader-follower relationship;
2. The context of leadership;
3. The processes of leadership

Almost all models or theories of leadership pay attention to the leader-follower relationship. Indeed, the very core of the idea is that followers need leaders and vice versa. Many models and theories go on to speculate about the characteristics or traits of leaders, and what separates leaders from followers. The academic research in this area is fairly clear: focusing on the characteristics or traits of a leader is not sufficient to separate leaders from followers. In other words, the "trait approach" or "great leader" approach doesn't tell us very much, even though such stories can be very useful in terms of generating insights and inspirational stories.

Other thinkers have studied the context of the leader-follower relationship. If understanding the traits of the leaders and followers didn't amount to much, maybe understanding their context or situations would help. We all know leaders that have excelled in some circumstances and been completely ineffective in other circumstances. A whole host of theories and models have been developed around situational or contextual or contingency models of leadership. The difficulty here is that the concepts of "context" or "situation" are just too broad. There are too many factors, and there are too many interactions with leadership traits.

More recent thinkers have begun to study the very processes of leadership: how leaders create commitment in followers, how they inspire others, how they reward and punish, and so on. A great many models focus on these processes, and some of these ideas have been developed into very practical models that categorize leadership styles or even leadership competencies.

THREE PROBLEMS WITH THE STANDARD IDEA OF LEADERSHIP

We want to suggest that this standard way of thinking about leadership suffers from three compelling drawbacks: (1) the problem of ethics, (2) the problem of authority, and (3) the problem of complexity. Let's look briefly at each one.

## The Problem of Ethics

Ethics and values generally find their way into these theories and models of leadership in one of two ways. The first we'll call "amoral leadership," the idea that ethics and values aren't really appropriate in thinking about leadership. The second we'll call "values-based leadership," which is concerned solely with the values (instead of the traits) of the leaders and followers. Both models have real problems.

One main part of the idea of leadership is that leaders get things done. Their effectiveness in getting things done is part of our evaluation of them as leaders. When this idea of effectiveness of achieving outcomes becomes the central feature of leadership, it is easy to lapse into thinking about leadership as amoral, concerned only with effectiveness and not the way things are done. Both Hitler and Gandhi were very effective in achieving organizational outcomes, but their methods, processes, relationship to followers, moral principles, and concern for others who were non-followers were very different. Merely saying that both were great leaders because they got things done is really not very interesting. It results in a view of leadership where ethics and values are minimized or just nonexistent.

Even if we look more closely at the leader-follower relationship and examine the values of each, we aren't much better off. Suppose that we take values as a central part of leadership, a kind of values-based leadership. The argument is that if we want to understand how an outcome emerged, then we have to understand the values of the leaders and followers. So, we check to see whether or not the leader was honest, trustworthy, and respectful (you can fill in your favorite set of values here) and we look to find the role that these values play in the determination of the outcomes. The leader either had good values or not. Or, we might look to see whether the values of the leader are aligned with those of the followers. Some of the more popular business thinkers like Jim Kouzes and Barry Posner, Stephen Covey, and Warren Bennis take this point of view.

The problem is that ethics is left out. How do we determine that a leader's values, even if shared by the followers, are good values? We need some critical process to distinguish the set of values that Hitler and his followers shared from those that are necessary to build sustainable institutions capable of helping us thrive in a global business environment. Values are an important part of this process, but sometimes values are not all warm and fuzzy. There are some pretty harsh values at work in the world, and we need an idea of leadership that does not tolerate cruelty and oppression but promotes freedom and the voluntary agreements that we make with each other. These are the ethical principles and values that have to underlie both capitalism and our idea of managing for stakeholders.

Leadership thinker and MacArthur Award winner Howard Gardner is one of the few who have written about this problem in a way that is applicable to today's business environment. He claims that "attention to leadership alone is sterile—and inappropriate. The larger topic of which leadership is a subtopic is the *accomplishment of group purposes.*"[1] Constraints to achieving the group purposes include the availability of resources, the degree of agreement as to basic values and objectives, the situation faced by leaders and followers, their willingness to adapt and renew, and issues of moral and social cohesion.

Gardner discusses the types of leaders that "clearly transgress our moral standards."[2] First, there are those leaders who use their followers for the leader's own ends and treat the followers with cruelty. Then there are those leaders who may treat their followers in an ethical way but who encourage them to do evil things. Some leaders exploit their followers' unconscious need for the all-powerful parent from early infancy, rendering them dependent and childlike. Other leaders appeal to our bigotry and our capacity for hatred. While we could think of examples of leaders that bear these characteristics in the extreme, it is important to remember that variations on these themes are relatively common.

The evaluation of immoral leaders is not confined to the leader. Gardner states, "It is easy to tell ourselves that in all of [these situations] . . . the sole source of evil was the leader. But the leader is never a sole causative factor. There is always, in some measure, the collaboration of those led. If a leader holds sway by exploiting our greed or our hatreds, the evil is in us too."[3] This leads us to the second problem with our standard idea about leadership.

### The Problem of Authority

Most executives in leadership positions have a problem that is so subtle that they are not aware of it. The problem is that the very idea of leadership is rigged. The game is fixed. Followers are naturally swayed by the authority of leaders. Followers will do, for the most part, what leaders tell them to do, regardless of what it is. Peer pressure works as an additional strong force.

Stanley Milgram, Philip Zimbardo, and other social psychologists have studied how the authority relationship works. In a historic set of experiments Milgram showed that with nothing at stake, more than 50 percent of people would deliver painful electric shocks to an innocent person when enmeshed in a situation driven by an authority figure. Milgram demonstrated that our default switch is set to obey authority, even with nothing at stake. Zimbardo followed this work with his famous prison experiments, where he showed that people will enact the social roles into which they are engaged. Tell a group that some will be prisoners and some will be guards, and they will literally create a prison-like situation. The default switch is to obey authority and enact the roles expected by leaders.

Most executives are enmeshed in the problem of authority, the social-psychological dynamics of obedience, peer pressure, and the socialization of doing what we are told. All things being equal, people simply do what they are told when they perceive the boss as a person with legitimate authority. The position of leader is often enough to command followers to act. Most leaders don't recognize the fact that their people doing what the leaders suggest has nothing to do with their brilliance, their values, or their ability to lead. People do what leaders suggest because of the authority of the leader.

At Miniscribe, a disk drive manufacturer in the 1980s, employees packed bricks into boxes and shipped them as disk drives. At Equity Funding, employees invented new identities for policy holders to keep a reinsurance scam afloat. At company after company employees implement directives that destroy value. Often they interpret the drive to achieve the numbers, the results, as an absolute directive, regardless of how it has to be done. Who can forget Adolf Eichman's defense at his trial in Jerusalem that he was just doing his job, just following orders?

Howard Gardner's idea of leadership is one of "leader by choice."[4] He claims that the only interesting idea is when followers actually choose to follow, and this means that followers must have adequate knowledge of alternatives and at least some options with respect to these alternatives. The implications for our idea of leadership in business are enormous. We depend a great deal on the authority of the office. The very idea of "boss" or "CEO" invokes the structure of authority and creates the presumption that the subordinate or follower will do what the boss says.

Not only do leaders have to figure out how to factor ethics and values into the center of their leadership, but they have to create situations whereby followers can engage in a genuine choice to follow them. This creates the third problem for our traditional conception of leadership: understanding the full range of human behavior.

## The Problem of Complexity

Most of our understanding of human behavior in business is built on an outdated model of how and why humans interact with each other in the process of value creation. The best way to say it is to recall a thought experiment proposed by the late managerial psychologist and analyst Harry Levinson. Levinson reflected on the use of the language of incentives, rewards, punishments, motivation, and other words that business executives and business thinkers use when they talk about people's behavior in organizations. Think about the carrot and the stick. Now picture in your mind a blank sheet of paper with a carrot on one end and a stick on the other. Levinson asked us to imagine what animal would most naturally fit in the picture. The overwhelming answer is a jackass or a donkey. We know that donkeys have to be coaxed ahead with a carrot (incentive) and beaten from behind with a stick (punishment).

Levinson made the simple observation that suppose human beings were in fact not like jackasses at all.[5] Suppose that they had rather complex psychologies and complicated physical, emotional, moral, and spiritual makeups. Imagine the damage that could be done if we designed organizational processes for jackasses, when in reality people were very different. The problem is deepened when we realize that if we treat people as jackasses, they may in fact start to act like the stubborn animals.

Here's another way to think about the problem. Suppose you have a theory about what makes people tick. Let's call it Theory I. Theory I, depicted in Figure 6.2, suggests that the most important element in explaining someone's behavior is the incentives that they believe were operating. If you believe Theory I, then you'll spend a lot time in business trying to create incentives for people, thinking about how incentives can be more directly tied to results or behavior and designing elaborate sets of rewards and punishments to go along with these incentives. Theory I, in fact, drives the human resource processes at many businesses.

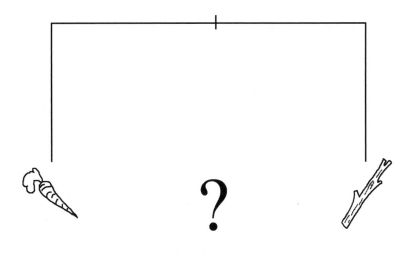

What Animal Is Between
the Carrot and the Stick?

**6.1. Levinson's thought experiment**

Consider a different theory about what makes people tick. Let's call it Theory V. Theory V, also depicted in Figure 6.2, says that what drives people to behave are their values, the most important principles, ideas, relationships, and things that are good in themselves. Of course, rewards and punishments play a role. It is important not to incentivize the wrong behavior, and it is important to see that the right behavior is rewarded, but that comes as an aftereffect of the process. It isn't the main driver. If Theory V is correct, then business leaders should spend a lot of time thinking through the purpose of their firms, the values and principles by which they want to create value for stakeholders, and whether or not these values are socially acceptable or represent social change. In other words, they should adopt what we have called here an enterprise approach.

*Incentives Drive Behavior: Theory I*

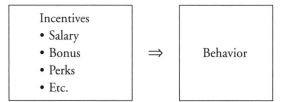

*Values Drive Behavior: Theory V*

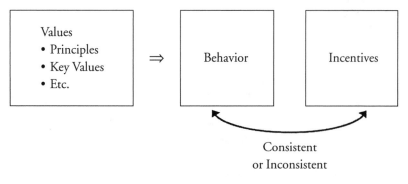

**6.2. Theory I and Theory V**

The important issue for understanding the problem of complexity isn't that we know that Theory I or Theory V is correct but to think through, as a leader, what your view is of why people do what they do. If you're a Theory I leader, you need to think about the cost of being wrong. If you're a Theory V leader, incentives are important, but you may have underestimated the importance of putting together the back end of the process (rewards and punishments) with the front end (values and principles). In either case you cannot avoid taking a stand on issues of ethics. Seeing people as jackasses is taking an ethical stance on the nature of our fellow human beings. Likewise, seeing people as complex economic, emotional, sexual, spiritual, and political beings is to take an ethical stance on the nature of humanity.

In summary, the problems of ethics, authority, and complexity tell us that we need some new ideas about leadership. These new ideas need to put a concern with ethics at the very center of our idea of leadership.

## THE IDEA OF ETHICAL LEADERSHIP

Will Miller is unusual for a corporate CEO. He has no problem talking about the purpose of his organization, the Irwin Financial Corporation, as "creating superior value for all of its stakeholders." Listening to Miller talk about some of the challenges that he has faced in his years at the helm, one is struck by his passion for the business that goes alongside his passion for doing the right thing. He simply doesn't see a conflict. He tells of a particularly troubling decision he once had to make and says that the answer was obvious once he understood that the right question was "twenty-five years from now, how would I have wanted to make this decision?"[6]

The guiding philosophy at Irwin is one that shows clear commitment to managing for stakeholders. Irwin people believe that stakeholders have a long list of things they want from Irwin and, naturally, the needs of stakeholders sometimes conflict with each other. Nevertheless, Irwin's stakeholders voluntarily make choices to associate with Irwin, so Irwin people have a responsibility to keep these relationships in balance and to constantly improve any tradeoffs that have to be made in the short term. The mission of Irwin, as articulated by Miller and other executives, is to "be the best financial services company through ethics and excellence, today and tomorrow." Will Miller and Irwin have some lessons to teach us about how to lead in a world that is filled with conflicting stakeholder demands.

In our experience we believe that ethical leadership resonates with most executives. They want to be effective and they want to leave the world a better place, creating value for those whose lives they touch. We have tried to elaborate this idea of ethical leadership along a number of different dimensions.

First, let's return to Howard Gardner and his idea of a morally acceptable leader. These leaders must have, at a minimum, the following objectives:

1. Releasing human potential of constituents
2. Balancing the needs of the individual and the community or organization
3. Defending the fundamental values of the community or organization
4. Instilling in individuals a sense of initiative and responsibility

Leadership, especially in large global organizations, is not confined to questions of the leader-follower relationship. The leader must work to eliminate or reduce some of the more dehumanizing aspects of large organizations. A key task of leadership, according to Gardner, is to devise ways to offset the inevitable tensions between largeness and control, vitality and creativity. Job redesign, autonomous working groups, schemes for performance feedback, and so on should be used to ensure that the constituents can find meaning in their work. Gardner characterizes these leadership tasks not as one means to enhancing organizational effectiveness but rather as a way to ensure the soundness of the organizational moral climate.

In addition, Gardner places an emphasis on the leader's role in setting a vision for the organization. Even in this fundamental task, we cannot separate leadership and values: "Leaders today are familiar with the demand that they come forward with a new vision. But it is not a matter of fabricating a new vision out of whole cloth. A vision relevant for us today will build on values deeply embedded in human history and in our own tradition. . . . The materials out of which we build the vision will be the moral strivings of the species, today and in the distant past."[7]

We can build on these ideas of Gardner and others to offer a view of the ethical leader and an ethical theory of leadership. In this view, little can be said about leadership without at least implicitly making moral or value judgments. Ethics and values pervade our ideas of leader-follower relationships, leadership context, as well as skills and processes. Followers make judgments and choices, project their wishes and dreams onto the leaders, and hold them accountable (or not). Situations are ripe with moral meaning, depending in part on how such contextual factors are framed. Processes cannot be divorced from the outcomes they produce and hence cannot be seen as morally neutral.

Ethical leadership also notes the social legitimacy (and hence the implicit value judgment) that is conferred on someone by simply calling her a leader. So the very idea of leadership cannot be stated without ethical judgment. Presumptively, leaders are legitimate—in business as well as the political sphere—and social legitimacy begins with the idea that one is acting from an ethical point of view.

### PRINCIPLES OF ETHICAL LEADERSHIP

We have tried to elaborate the idea of ethical leadership into a core set of principles, and a set of practical behaviors for executives. What are the core principles of ethical leadership?

### The Leader Principle

A leader is first and foremost a member of her own organization and stakeholder group. As such, her actions, goals, and interactions are for the benefit of the entire group of stakeholders.

### The Constituents Principle

Leaders see their constituents as more than followers—rather as stakeholders to the common purpose and vision. They have their own individuality and autonomy that is respected in order to maintain a moral community.

### The Outcome Principle

A leader embodies the purpose and values of the organization and of the constituents within an understanding of ethical ideals. A leader connects the basic value proposition to stakeholder support and societal legitimacy. He connects the goals of the organization with that of the internal individuals and external constituents.

### The Processes/Skills Principle

A leader works to create an open, two-way conversation, thereby maintaining a charitable understanding of different views, values, and opinions of her constituents. She is open to others' opinions and ideas.

### The Situation/Context Principle

A leader sees particular values and ethical principles as being useful within certain spheres. He uses moral imagination to make difficult decisions to cross the boundaries of those spheres and the frontiers of knowledge.[8]

### The Ethics Principle

A leader frames actions and purposes in ethical terms. A leader does not understand leadership without ethics but rather thinks in terms of consequences, principles, rights, as well as character in her actions, beliefs, and behaviors. A leader takes responsibility for the effects of her actions on others.

#### THE TASKS OF ETHICAL LEADERSHIP

It's time to put together the analysis of the previous sections into some concrete tasks for executives who must manage in the turbulent world of today—who must devote their time and energy into leading the process of value creation. The argument has been that such a process has ethics and values present at a number of levels. In fact, it would be disingenuous to try to separate out which tasks are ethical ones and which are business ones, for the idea behind managing for stakeholders is that one can't and shouldn't separate business from ethics. Ethical leadership frees leaders to incorporate and be explicit about their own values and ethics.

The following set of tasks is based on the observations of and conversations with a host of executives and students over the past twenty-five years and on a reading of the business literature, both popular and scholarly. It should, however, be seen as tentative and open to revision. The set of tasks is from the perspective of the leader—what the leader should do to incorporate the principles from above and embody ethical leadership. The tasks are displayed through the lens of the canonical model to demonstrate how the ethical leader deals with each facet of ethical leadership.

*Ethical leaders articulate and embody the purpose and values of the organization.* It is important for leaders to tell a compelling and morally rich story, but ethical leaders must also embody and live the story. This is a difficult task in today's business environment where everyone lives in a fishbowl—on public display. So many political leaders fail to embody the high-minded stories they tell at election time, and more recently, business leaders have become the focus of similar criticism through the revelations of numerous scandals and bad behaviors. CEOs in today's corporations are really ethical role models for all of society. Following a series of unethical activities by Citigroup in Japan in 2004, CEO Chuck Prince fired several executives, publicly accepted responsibility, and bowed apologetically to Japanese officials.[9] Not only did Prince's message resonate within Japan, but it also signaled a new era of shared responsibility within the culture of Citigroup, where all employees were expected to take ownership for their decisions that affected the enterprise.

*Ethical leaders focus on organizational success rather than on personal ego.* Ethical leaders understand their place within the larger network of constituents and stakeholders. It is not about the leader as an individual; it is about something bigger—the goals and dreams of the organization. Ethical leaders also recognize that value is in the success of people in the organization. In 1998, in a bold gesture demonstrating how he valued the company's line employees, Roger Enrico, former chairman and CEO of PepsiCo, chose to forego all but $1 of his salary, requesting that PepsiCo, in turn, contribute $1 million to a scholarship fund for employees' children.[10] In a similar manner, the founders of JetBlue began a process of matching, from their salaries, employee donations to a charity. Today, their entire salaries go to the JetBlue Crewmember Catastrophic Plan charity, to assist staff with crises not covered by insurance.[11] The point of these examples is not that ethical leaders donate their salaries to charities but rather that ethical leaders identify and act on levers, such as employee loyalty, that drive organizational success.

*Ethical leaders find the best people and develop them.* This task is fairly standard in different models of leadership. Ethical leaders pay special attention to finding and developing the best people precisely because they see it as a moral imperative—helping them to lead better lives that create more value for themselves and for others. Finding the best people involves taking ethics and character into account in the selection process. Many CEOs have said to us that judging someone's integrity is far more important than evaluating their experience and skills. Yet in many organizations, employees are hired to fill a particular skill need with little regard to issues of integrity.

*Ethical leaders create a conversation about ethics, values, and the creation of value for stakeholders that is alive.* Too often business executives think that having a laminated values card in their wallet or purely having a compliance approach to ethics has solved the ethics problem. Suffice it to say that Enron and other troubled companies had these systems in place. What they didn't have was a conversation across all levels of the business where the basics of value creation, stakeholder principles, and societal expectations were routinely discussed and debated. There is a fallacy that values and ethics are the soft, squishy part of management. Nothing could be further from the truth.

In organizations that have a live conversation about ethics and values, people hold each other responsible and accountable about whether they are really living the values. They expect the leaders of the organization to do the same. Bringing such a conversation to life means that people must have knowledge of alternatives, and they must choose every day to stay with the organization and its purpose because it is important and inspires them. Making a strong commitment to bringing this conversation to life is essential to do if one is to lead ethically.

Most people know the story of Johnson and Johnson's Jim Burke and the Tylenol product recall in the 1980s in which, at a great short-term financial cost, he pulled all potentially tampered-with products off the shelves, thereby keeping the public's trust intact. The background is that Johnson and Johnson had held a series of challenge meetings all around the world, where managers sat and debated their credo, a statement of their purpose and principles. The conversation about ethics at Johnson and Johnson was alive and in many ways made Jim Burke's choice about handling the situation clearer than it otherwise would have been.

*Ethical leaders create mechanisms of dissent.* Many executives don't realize how powerful they are simply by virtue of their positions. The research on the authority relationship, described earlier, has long ago demonstrated that most of the time people will obey what they perceive to be legitimate authority, even if there is no cost for disobedience. To avoid this authority trap it is critical to have an established and explicit way to push back if someone thinks that a particular market, region, or internal process is out of line. This needs to be beyond a compliance approach to ethics. Some companies have used anonymous e-mail and telephone processes to give employees a way around the levels of management that inevitably spring up as barriers in large organizations. Many executives also have used "skip level" meetings where they go down multiple levels in the organization to get a more realistic view of what is actually going on. General Electric's famous "workout" process —where workers meet to decide how to fix problems and make the company better—was a way for front-line employees to push back against the established policies and authority of management. All of these processes lead to better decisions, more engaged employees, and an increased likelihood of avoiding mistakes.

In a company that takes its purpose or values seriously, there must be mechanisms of pushing back to avoid the values becoming stale and dead. Indeed, many of the current corporate scandals could have been prevented if only there were more creative ways for people to express their dissatisfaction with the actions of some of their leaders and others in the companies. The process of developing these mechanisms of dissent will vary by company, by leadership style, and by culture, but it is a crucial leadership task for value creation in today's business world.

*Ethical leaders take a charitable understanding of others' values.* Ethical leaders can understand why different people make different choices but still have a strong grasp on what they would do and why. Following twenty-seven years in South African prisons, Nelson Mandela was still able to see the good in his jailers. After one particularly vicious jailer was being transferred away from Robben Island because of Mandela's protest and push back, the jailer turned to Mandela and stated, "I just want to wish you people good luck."[12] Mandela interpreted this statement charitably as a sign that all people had some good within them, even those caught up in an evil system. Mandela felt that it was his responsibility to see this good in people and to try and bring it out. One CEO suggested that instead of seeing ethical leadership as preventing people from doing the wrong thing, we need to view it as enabling people to do the right thing.

*Ethical leaders make tough calls while being imaginative.* Ethical leaders inevitably have to make a lot of difficult decisions, from reorienting the company's strategy and basic value proposition to making individual personnel decisions such as working with employees exiting the organization. Ethical leaders do not attempt to avoid difficult decisions with the excuse, "I'm doing this for the business." The ethical leader consistently puts together "doing the right thing" and "doing the right thing for the business."

The idea that ethical leadership is just being nice is far from the truth. Often, exercising "moral imagination" is the most important task.[13] Mohammed Yunus founded the Grameen Bank on such moral imagination.[14] By taking the standard banking practice of only lending to people with collateral, and turning it on its head, Yunus spawned an industry of micro-lending to the poor. Grameen Bank's motto is that poverty belongs in a museum. In addition to having one of the highest loan repayment rates in the banking industry, the bank's program of lending to poor women in Bangladesh to start businesses has helped millions to be able to feed themselves.

This leadership can just as often take place within the ranks of organizations as it does at the highest CEO and board levels. Several years ago, the chairman of a major chemical company was implementing a new, stringent company-wide commitment to reduce factory emissions.[15] He visited one facility where the plant engineers insisted that such requirements could not be met. The chairman responded that the particular plant would then have to be closed—causing hundreds of job losses. Several weeks later, the plant engineers delivered the news to the chairman that they had figured out how to meet the requirements—and save money. While we don't know the names of the plant engineers who surely spent numerous hours determining how to meet the requirements, we see the results of their leadership and imagination.

*Ethical leaders know the limits of the values and ethical principles they live.* All values have limits, particular spheres in which they do not work as well as others. The limits for certain values, for instance, may be related to the context or the audience in which they are being used. Ethical leaders have an acute sense of the limits of the values they live and are prepared with solid reasons to defend their chosen course of action. Problems can arise when managers do not understand the limits of certain values. As an example, one issue common to all of the recent scandals was that managers and executives did not understand the limits of putting shareholders first. Attempts to artificially keep stock prices high—without creating any lasting value for customers and other stakeholders—can border on fanaticism rather than good judgment. Ethics is no different from any other part of our lives: there is no substitute for good judgment, sound advice, practical sense, and conversations with those affected by our actions.

*Ethical leaders frame actions in ethical terms.* Ethical leaders see their leadership as a fully ethical task. This entails taking seriously the rights claims of others, considering the effects of one's actions on others (stakeholders), and understanding how acting or leading in a certain way will have effects on one's character and the character of others. There is nothing amoral about ethical leaders, and they recognize that their own values may sometimes turn out to be a poor guidepost.

The ethical leader takes responsibility for using sound moral judgment, but there is a caution here. It is easy to frame actions in ethical terms and be perceived as righteous. Many have the view that ethics is about universal, inviolable principles that are carved into stone. We need to start with principles and values and then work hard to figure out how they can be applied in today's complex global business environment. Principles, values, cultures, and individual differences often conflict. Ethical leadership requires an attitude of humility rather than righteousness: a commitment to one's own principles and at the same time openness to learning and to having conversations with others who may have a different way of seeing the world. Ethics is best viewed as an open conversation about those values and issues that are most important to us and to our business. It is a continual discovery and reaffirmation of our own principles and values, and a realization that we can improve through encountering new ideas.

*Ethical leaders connect the basic value proposition to stakeholder support and societal legitimacy.* The ethical leader must think in terms of enterprise strategy, not separating business from ethics. Linking the basic raison d'être of the enterprise with the way that value gets created and society's expectations is a gargantuan task, but the ethical leader never hides behind the excuse of "it's just business."

Despite intense opposition from a number of groups, Wal-Mart CEO Lee Scott won approval in early 2004 to build a new store in a West Side Chicago neighborhood by listening to and engaging stakeholders who would most benefit by the value that this new store would create.[16] Partnering with black community leaders, Wal-Mart appealed to the needs of the community in sections of town where there was a real need for jobs and stores. Ultimately, the support of the community allowed Wal-Mart to win the approval of the city council. Wal-Mart also committed to seeking minority subcontractors to build the facility and to eventually hire the majority of the store's employees from the local community.

Ethical leadership is about raising the bar, helping people to realize their hopes and dreams, creating value for stakeholders, and doing these tasks with the intensity and importance that "ethics" connotes. That said, there must be room for mistakes, for humor, and for a humanity that is sometimes missing in our current leaders. Ethical leaders are ordinary people who are living their lives as examples of making the world a better place while reaping benefits for themselves. Ethical leaders speak to us about our identity, what we are and what we can become, how we live and how we could live better.

### BECOMING AN ETHICAL LEADER

We have been privileged to know many executives that we would classify as ethical leaders. What these people have in common is a profound and deep sense of ethical principles, values, and character at the core of their leadership. They see their job as making others better and enabling them to pursue their own hopes and dreams. They are able to get things done in complicated organizations and societies. But it is their ethical core that pervades their relationships with followers, the skills and processes that they use in leading them, their analysis of the contexts, and their own sense of self.

Becoming an ethical leader is really fairly simple. It is a commitment to examining your own behavior, your own values, and the dedication to accept the responsibility for the effects of your actions on others as well as yourself.

Such a responsibility principle is a necessary ingredient if managing for stakeholders is to have any usefulness in today's business world. If business is just about shareholder value, then responsibility has no place, other than responsibility to shareholders. What about all of the other effects of our actions on customers, suppliers, employees, communities, and other stakeholders?

Becoming an ethical leader is no easier or harder than committing to ask the following kinds of questions. There are many other possibilities that you can add for yourself:

1. What are my most important values and principles?

2. Does my calendar, how I spend my time and attention, reflect these values?

3. What would my subordinates and peers say my values are?

4. What mechanisms and processes have I designed to be sure that the people who work for me can push back against my authority?

5. What could this organization do or ask me to do that would cause me to resign for ethical reasons?

6. What do I want to accomplish with my leadership?

7. What do I want people to say about my leadership when I am gone?

8. Can I go home at the end of the day and tell my children (or a loved one) about my leadership, and use my day's work to teach them to be ethical leaders?

### DEVELOPING ETHICAL LEADERS

The best way for an organization to develop ethical leaders, we believe, is to engage in some of the questions we have suggested in this book. Trying to begin to see business simultaneously in economic and ethical terms goes a long way toward sending the message that ethics isn't just an important set of rules not to violate, it is part and parcel of what it means to work at an organization.

There are some concrete steps, in our opinion, about how best to develop ethical leaders within the framework that most global businesses find themselves. The first step is to bring to life a conversation about how the organization makes its stakeholders better off and what its values are. This doesn't need to be a program. It can be as elaborate as town hall meetings. Or, as one executive suggested to us, we could have an ethics or stakeholders moment at most meetings. Such a moment, analogous to "safety moments" at companies like DuPont, sets aside a brief time to raise concerns about the effects of the meeting on key stakeholders, or on a company's values and ethics. Equally, the ethics moment could elaborate on how the conversations and decisions of the meeting were aligned with what the company stands for.

Many companies have leadership development programs. These programs need to be strengthened by adding the idea of ethical leadership. You need not use the specific principles we have developed, but it is useful to engage the participants in a conversation about what they see as ethical leadership. Executives can develop shared conversations and conceptions of how ethical leadership can be implemented in their particular company.

Executives need to figure out how to have challenge meetings, routine processes where anyone in the organization can raise a challenge to whether or not the company is living its values or its enterprise approach. Many fear that anarchy would be the result of such a process. Our experience is just the opposite. Values, purposes, principles, an enterprise approach, all deliver a disciplined way to think about how to make the business better and more effective, as well as something that everyone can be proud of. Without the ability to challenge authority, there really can be no such thing as ethical leadership.

We have asked a lot of Bob Collingwood and his colleagues—and of you. We have suggested that we need a new mindset about business, and that mindset must put business and ethics together. The new mindset must focus on stakeholders—that is, at least customers, suppliers, employees, communities, and financiers. We must see business as managing for stakeholders. We ask for no less than a revision to the capitalist framework. Business just is creating value for stakeholders. If you see it like that, there is a great deal of change that needs to be done.

We have suggested several ways, and sets of questions to ask, to facilitate this change. Ultimately, we believe that such change is very easy. If we are clear about what we stand for, then changing how we think about business is not difficult so long as it is aligned with our values. We have argued that ethical leadership must be at the heart of this change.

Business has lost the public trust. By managing for stakeholders we can regain this vital asset and leave the generations that follow with a vision of business that places value creation for stakeholders at the center. There is a great deal at stake here. With trust, business will be a more effective force in alleviating human suffering, in lifting millions of people out of poverty, in creating products and services that make our lives better—and in creating financial value for shareholders. We have a real opportunity to be the generation that makes capitalism better. The choice is ours.

# Appendix: Frequently Asked Questions about Managing for Stakeholders (MFS)

1. Is managing for stakeholders opposed to maximizing value for shareholders? Don't the interests of shareholders and stakeholders conflict?

Shareholders are an important stakeholder, so we can't understand MFS as anti-shareholder or against the interests of shareholders. Without the support of the folks and institutions that put up the money, a business can't exist. However, we do believe that if managers try to maximize the interests of any one stakeholder, they will run into trouble. Maximizing the interests of one group, in essence, trades off the interests of others against the group being maximized. MFS is not about tradeoff thinking. It is about using innovation and entrepreneurship to make all key stakeholders better off, to get all of their interests going in the same direction. Maximizing the interests of one group gives a false sense of security in a complex world where we have a limited ability to predict what will happen (what economists call "bounded rationality"). Even if you wanted to maximize shareholder value, we believe you would do so by creating great products for customers, having suppliers committed to making your firm better, having employees who are engaged in their work, and being good citizens in the community (at least to avoid punitive actions by the community). In short, you would be creating value for stakeholders, or managing for stakeholders.

2. Can we really make all of the stakeholders happy all of the time?

Absolutely not. You must have a clear sense of what you stand for and how you are going to make your key stakeholders better off. You need to get the interests of primary stakeholders, at least customers, suppliers, employees, communities, and financiers (for most companies), going in the same direction, most of the time. And, you can't ignore the other stakeholders such as media, critics, governments, NGOs, and so on, but you can't always satisfy all of their interests. The key is your mindset. You have to see even the harshest critics as potential sources of valuable insight and innovation about your business. MFS is about engaging stakeholders, innovation, and the creation of value.

3. Is managing for stakeholders just another way to say "corporate social responsibility," "triple bottom line," or "sustainable business?" What is the connection among these ideas?

We have a lot in common with those thinkers who want to use ideas like "corporate social responsibility" and "triple bottom line" to create a new understanding about business and capitalism. Like us, they want businesses to be responsible for the effects of their actions on others, and they see these effects as much broader than effects on shareholders. The problem with these ideas, however, is that they make a distinction between the economic or business effects of an action and its social effects. Within the current model of business it is too easy to relegate social effects to corporate philanthropy or public relations, or some other second-rate status. We believe that by starting with stakeholders we can see how economic and social and other effects go together.

Starting with stakeholders is just a better unit of analysis than either social responsibility or triple bottom line.

4. What is the connection between managing for stakeholders and ethics in business?

MFS requires that we see stakeholders as fully human. Customers are not just "buyers" and employees are not just "human resources." They are people with names, faces, children, hopes, and desires, subject to the same complexity and foibles as all of us. Capitalism works because of this humanity. It is our way of cooperating to achieve common purposes. Ethics is inseparable from this endeavor, as it is about how we are going to live together and thrive. Ethics is about the principles that allow us to live together and the values that we share. It is also about the limits of tolerance and the limitations we place on ourselves to ensure a smooth-functioning society. The idea that business and ethics are not connected or that business ethics is a joke is a dehumanizing idea. A better question might be, "how did we ever believe that business and ethics were not connected . . . how did we get that so wrong?"

5. Why worry about managing for stakeholders now?

The forces of globalization, the emergence of liberal democracies and the end of centralized planning, and the explosion of information technology have all contributed to the demise of the standard way of thinking about business as primarily concerned with shareholders. Managers need a framework, a mindset, a worldview that routinely understands these changes and helps them to make better decisions. Managing for stakeholders is a simple way to understand a complex world. It says to first understand who is affected by your actions and how they are affected. Understand what you stand for and the kind of company you want to build so that you will have a base to work from as the world gets complicated. It says that even if you want to maximize shareholder value, you have to think about stakeholders and how you create value for customers, employees, suppliers, and communities, as well as financiers.

6. Does managing for stakeholders work well in the long term but not so well in the short term?

We believe that MFS works in the short term. Each stakeholder relationship must be managed in such a way that it creates value in the short term yet preserves the idea that value creation is going to continue into the long term. Great products with inspired employees, committed suppliers, and satisfied communities and shareholders produce real, tangible value in the here and now. The idea that thinking about stakeholders pays only in the long term makes the mistake of seeing stakeholder interests as opposed to shareholder interests. If anything pays off in the long term, there must be some time at which it begins to pay off and hence pays in the short term as well. Good long-term performance is just sustained good short-term performance. By focusing on creating value for all stakeholders and keeping their interests going in the same direction, we can merge the short term into the long term. Ultimately, the tradeoff between "short term" and "long term" is not a robust way to think about business. Anyone can justify most any decision by saying either that it will work in the long term, or it had to be done for the short term. Figuring out good decisions that work in both is a better approach, and we believe that MFS facilitates that process.

7. How will managing for stakeholders help rebuild the public trust in business and capitalism after the Enron debacle?

We need a new narrative, a new story about business. Enron and the other scandals reinforce the idea that capitalism is morally evil, and that businesspeople are morally shady or of questionable character. We misunderstand both business and ethics. Business is not about making as much money as possible. It is about creating value for stakeholders. It is important to say this and to enable business people to enact this story. We need to hold up the 10,000 companies, large and small, that are out there trying to do the right thing for their stakeholders, as the real paradigm of business, rather than deeply flawed companies like Enron. We misunderstand ethics because it must be at the center of our lives in business and outside of business. Ethics is about the conversations we have with each other about how we are going to live, and this includes what kinds of businesses we are going to create. The real mistake is separating business from ethics. MFS puts these ideas together clearly. Asking the questions, "What do we stand for?" "How are we going to make stakeholders better off?" and "What values and principles can we use to manage these relationships over time?" connects business and ethics once and for all.

8. How do you identify stakeholders? Isn't everybody a stakeholder in large multinational companies? Why are companies in the center of the stakeholder map?

The best way to identify stakeholders, in our opinion, is to convene a diverse group of people from an organization and ask them who is affected by the organization and who can affect the organization. In our experience executives easily identify and prioritize stakeholders. The only problem is that there is a tendency not to listen to groups that are critical of the company. And, yes, large multinationals have lots of stakeholders, but stakeholders can be stratified by what part of the business they affect. We prefer to see stakeholders as concrete groups and individuals rather than large amorphous groups like "the public" or "society." Such large groups have so little in common; there are very few strategies to use to influence society or the public at large.

9. Is managing for stakeholders just for business? What about non-profits?

It is fairly easy to apply MFS to nonprofits as well. The fact is that MFS describes how we create value for each other, and how we account for that value is in part irrelevant. Nonprofits are also trying to create value for stakeholders. While the particular stakeholders may be different from for-profit corporations, the idea that the nonprofit manager has to get these stakeholder interests going in the same direction is the same. Too many nonprofits believe that they are different from business. Because they mean well and intend to do good they should be exempt from the responsibility to create value for their stakeholders. We believe that a stakeholder approach to nonprofits brings the discipline of a business approach to the problem together with the good intentions to do good for civil society.

10. In my job I rarely deal with people outside my company. Can I apply some of the techniques and ideas to internal stakeholders?

Back in the 1970s when it was less evident that the stakeholder approach was needed, many executives tried to apply the idea to internal stake-holders. After all, they claimed, the external environment was pretty stable. That's not a bad idea. You can put yourself into the center of a stakeholder map and look at who is affected by your doing your job, and who can affect you as you do your job. The idea of personal stakeholders is valid. The only problem is that when you work for a company you must ultimately touch someone who is external. It is dangerous for everyone in a company to be very stakeholder-oriented to each other but ignore the external world. In the twenty-first century, businesses must take a radically external view. They must be responsive to external stakeholders. By paying attention to only internal stakeholders there can be a problem. This is especially true during the merger and acquisition process. At exactly the time that a company needs to pay attention to external stakeholders, often what happens is that the managers focus on internal stakeholders for reasons of job security, influence, and power. Internal stakeholders can be valid, as long as they are combined with some external stakeholders as well.

# Notes

CHAPTER 1: MANAGING FOR STAKEHOLDERS

1. "Economic value added" is a measure that calculates on a project-by-project basis the effects of a particular investment on the stock price. For an explanation of EVA, see Robert F. Bruner et al., *The Portable MBA,* 4th ed. (New York: John Wiley and Sons, 2003).

2. Bob Collingwood is an amalgam of the thousands of executives with whom we have engaged in conversations about the issues raised in this book. While none of them are exactly Bob Collingwood, most of them will recognize the pressures he faces. If this set of pressures seems extreme, imagine Bob's counterpart, Nan, who must cope with all of Bob's issues as well as issues of gender, or suppose that Bob is not a member of the dominant ethnicity or culture.

3. The origin of the idea of managing for stakeholders is complex. For one view, see chapter 2 of R. Edward Freeman, *Strategic Management: A Stakeholder Approach* (Boston: Pitman, 1984). For a related view, see Giles Slinger, "Essays on Stakeholding" (Ph.D. diss., Cambridge University, Department of Applied Economics, 1999). For an idiosyncratic account of Freeman's role in the development of the idea, see R. Edward Freeman, "The Development of Stakeholder Theory," in Ken Smith and Michael Hitt (eds.), *Great Minds in Management,* (Oxford, U.K.: Oxford University Press, 2005).

4. There are many ways to depict stakeholders. We follow Robert Phillips, *Stakeholder Theory and Organization Ethics*, here.

5. It could even depict the world in which shareholders are the "most legitimate" stakeholders, simply by restricting the primary stakeholders circle to shareholders, making all others instrumental or secondary stakeholders.

6. This number is for 2006 according to the Social Investment Forum, *http:// www.socialinvest.org/areas/general/investors/individuals.htm,* accessed on March 6, 2007. While the precise number is almost impossible to obtain, it is clear that this is a growing area of investment.

7. Bill George, *Authentic Leadership* (San Francisco, Calif.: Jossey-Bass, 2003), p. 104.

8. Like many good ideas in management, enterprise strategy was initially articulated by Peter Drucker in *The Concept of the Corporation* (New York: John Day and Co., 1972), as well as in his *Management: Tasks, Responsibilities, Practices* (New York: Harper and Row, 1974) as far as we can tell.

9. Robert A. Phillips and Craig B. Caldwell, "Value Chain Responsibility: A Farewell to Arm's Length," *Business & Society Review* 110, no. 4 (2005): 345–70.

### CHAPTER 2: BUSINESS IN THE TWENTY-FIRST CENTURY

1. The difference between managerial and shareholder capitalism is large. The existence of agency theory, however, lets us treat the two identically for our purposes here. Both agree on the view that the modern firm is characterized by the separation of decision making and residual risk bearing. The resulting agency problem is the subject of a vast literature. See Norman E. Bowie and R. Edward Freeman, *Ethics and Agency Theory: An Introduction* (New York: Oxford University Press, 1992) for an introduction to these issues.

2. Alfred Chandler's brilliant book *Strategy and Structure* (Cambridge, Mass.: MIT Press, 1962) chronicles the rise of the divisionalized corporation. For a not-so-flattering account of General Motors during the same time period, see Peter Drucker's classic work *The Concept of the Corporation* (New York: Harper and Row, 1974).

3. This is a tremendously stylized and oversimplified history. For a more careful analysis, see Allen Kaufman, Lawrence Zacharias, and Marvin Carson, *Managers*

*vs. Owners: The Struggle for Corporate Control in American Democracy* (New York: Oxford University Press, 1995).

4. This view was articulated as an argument against the stakeholder view by no less a personage than T. Boone Pickens, on the public television program *Business Ethics Roundtable,* produced by WVET in New York, 1992.

5. See Business Roundtable Institute for Corporate Ethics, *Mapping the Terrain Study. http://www.corporate-ethics.org*; accessed March 6, 2007.

### CHAPTER 3: THE BASIC FRAMEWORK

1. Such a "names and faces" approach to managing for stakeholders is set forth in John McVea and R. Edward Freeman, "Stakeholder Theory: A Names and Faces Approach," *Journal of Management Inquiry* 14, no. 1 (2005).

### CHAPTER 4: STAKEHOLDERS, PURPOSE, AND VALUES

1. From *www.abbott.com/citizenship/pdf/Supplier_Code_of_Conduct.pdf.* All subsequent quotes from Abbott's statement are taken from here, accessed March 6, 2007.

2. See Irwin Financial Corporation, Statement of Guiding Philosophy, 2006 edition. *http://www.irwinfinancial.com/cp-set.html,* accessed on March 5, 2007.

3. The Whole Foods Market "Declaration of Interdependence" can be found at *www.wholefoodsmarket.com/company/declaration.html,* accessed on March 6, 2007. In addition, see CEO John Mackey's blog at the same site on "Conscious Capitalism." The ideas there are quite consistent with most of the ideas in this book.

4. Information on Novo Nordisk can be found at *http://www.novonordisk-us.com/documents/home_page/document/index.asp,* accessed March 6, 2007. We are also grateful for helpful conversations with the Novo Nordisk stakeholder engagement team in Copenhagen in 2005.

### CHAPTER 5: EVERYDAY STRATEGIES FOR CREATING VALUE FOR STAKEHOLDERS

1. There are many companies whose business is built around doing "stakeholder assessments," or who have such a tool as a line of business. Often these assessments

come at the beginning of a project on "stakeholder engagement." Our purpose here is to set forth the underlying logic for many specific processes that managers can build for their own companies.

## CHAPTER 6: LEADERSHIP AND MANAGING FOR STAKEHOLDERS

1. Howard Gardner, *Leading Minds* (New York: Basic Books, 1995), p. xvi.

2. Gardner, *Leading Minds,* p. 67.

3. Gardner, *Leading Minds,* p. 71.

4. Gardner, *Leading Minds.*

5. Harry Levinson, *The Great Jackass Fallacy* (Cambridge, Mass.: Harvard University Press, 1973).

6. These passages about Irwin Financial Corporation are based on a number of speeches and classes given at the Darden School by Will Miller and Matt Souza over the last ten years. They are referenced here with permission of Irwin Financial Corporation.

7. Gardner, *Leading Minds,* p. xi.

8. "Moral imagination refers to the ability to perceive that a web of competing economic relationships is, at the same time, a web of moral relationships. Developing moral imagination means becoming sensitive to ethical issues in business decision making, but it also means searching out places where people are likely to be hurt by decision making or behavior of managers. This moral imagination is a necessary first step, but because of prevailing methods of evaluating managers on bottom-line results, it is extremely challenging." Patricia Werhane, *Moral Imagination and Moral Decision Making* (New York: Oxford University Press, 1999), 5.

9. Information for this section collected from: Carol J. Loomis and Chuck Prince, "Tough Questions for Citigroup's CEO," *Fortune,* November 29, 2004; and Timothy L. O'Brien and Landon Thomas Jr., "It's Cleanup Time at Citi," *New York Times,* November 7, 2004.

10. "Boss Gives His Salary to Workers Pepsi Chief Funds $1M in Scholarships," Associated Press, March 25, 1998.

11. James Wynbrandt, *Flying High: How JetBlue Founder and CEO David Neeleman Beats the Competition . . . Even in the World's Most Turbulent Industry* (New York: John Wiley and Sons, 2004), pp. 221–22.

12. Nelson Mandela, *The Long Walk To Freedom: The Autobiography of Nelson Mandela* (Boston: Little Brown and Co., 1994), p. 462.

13. Patricia H. Werhane, *Moral Imagination and Management Decision Making* (New York: Oxford University Press, 1999).

14. Mohammed Yunus, founder of the Grameen Bank, from a speech at the Ruffin Lecture Series of the Olsson Center for Applied Ethics at the University of Virginia's Darden School of Business, November 20, 2004.

15. R. Edward Freeman, Jessica Pierce, and Richard H. Dodd, *Environmentalism and the New Logic of Business: How Firms Can Be Profitable and Leave Our Children a Living Planet* (New York: Oxford University Press, 2000), p. 1.

16. *Time,* September 5, 2005, pp. 44–49; and on MSNBC.com, "Chicago Approves its First Wal-Mart: After Lengthy Debate, City Council Votes to Allow Store," *Associated Press,* May 26, 2004.

# Further Reading

There are a number of recent books and articles on managing for stakeholders, even though their terminology may be a bit different. We have drawn on all of these sources for *Managing for Stakeholders*. In addition to these sources, there are hundreds of academic and practical articles that have been written over the past thirty years. A simple Google search on "stakeholder management" yields 5.5 million hits, many of which contain interesting and useful ideas. In particular we recommend:

Donaldson, Thomas, and Lee Preston. "The Stakeholder Theory of the Corporation: Concepts, Evidence, and Implications." *Academy of Management Review* 20 (1994): 65–91.

The authors review the academic literature on managing for stakeholders.

Freeman, R. Edward. *Strategic Management: A Stakeholder Approach.* Boston: Pitman Publishing, 1984.

This long-out-of-print book can now be downloaded from Web sites of the Business Roundtable Institute for Corporate Ethics and the Olsson Center for Applied Ethics at the Darden School, University of Virginia. See *http:// www.corporate-ethics.org* and *http://www.darden.virginia.edu/html/area.aspx?style id=3&area=olsson.*

Phillips, Robert. *Stakeholder Theory and Organizational Ethics.* San Francisco: Berret-Koehler, 2003.

This book focuses explicitly on the connection between managing for stakeholders and ethics. It proposes a concrete and practical test about whether stakeholders are treated fairly, and how a company can determine whether or not it should satisfy a stakeholder's demands.

Post, James, Lee Preston, and Sybille Sachs. *Redefining the Corporation: Stakeholder Management and Organizational Wealth.* Palo Alto, Calif.: Stanford University Press, 2002.

This book focuses on several case studies of companies that are creating value by managing for stakeholders. It contains a practical criterion for determining who is and who is not a stakeholder, based on the risks and resources.

Svendson, Ann. *The Stakeholder Strategy: Profiting from Collaborative Business Relationships.* San Francisco, Calif.: Berret-Koehler, 1998.

The author explains the role of collaboration and collaborative strategy in managing for stakeholders. In particular she focuses on the need to get multiple stakeholder collaboration. Companies such as The Body Shop, Glaxo Wellcome, British Petroleum, Levi Strauss, and others are analyzed.

Wheeler, David, and Maria Sillanpaa. *The Stakeholder Corporation.* London: Pitman Publishing, 1997.

This book is an account of the stakeholder model as developed at The Body Shop by two executives who worked on implementing the ideas in the real world. It contains many useful ideas, especially at the level of key business processes oriented toward stakeholders and transactions at the day-to-day level. There are examples from the entirety of the business world as their version of managing for stakeholders is developed.

Wicks, Andrew, and R. Edward Freeman. "Organization Studies and the New Pragmatism: Positivism, Anti-positivism, and the Search for Ethics." *Organization Science* 9 (1998): 123–40.

This paper describes the method that we have used in this book. Its focus on "pragmatism" and the development of new narratives or stories about business is controversial in the business disciplines.

# Index

Page numbers in italic refer to illustrations.

strategic intent, 78

*Strategic Management: A Stakeholder Approach* (Freeman), 165

strategic thinking: 66, 75–79, 116; element of enterprise strategy, 19; need for focus on stakeholder relationships, 69; public relations, inclusion in, 125; stakeholder approach, 59, 104–105; transformed into stakeholder thinking, 73

strategies, defensive, 121

strategy. *See* enterprise strategy

*Strategy and Structure* (Chandler), 166

suppliers, *25;* in responsibility chain, *14;* as stakeholder, *7, 51;* in value chain, *14*

Svendson, Ann, 172

3M, 9, 28, 59, 76

trade organizations, 121–122

transactions: with activists, 119; market, 56; with stakeholders, 19, 61, 70–72, 117, 124, 128–130, 172

Tylenol, 149

Unipart Group, 95

United Technologies, 67–68

value chain, *14,* 15, 32

value creation, general, viii, 6, 11, 12, 13, 16, 19, 69, 70, 71, 109–111, 113, 116, *117,* 124, 125, 128, 148, 150, 156, 160; activities, 74; capitalism, 21; center of the business, 70; enterprise strat-

egy, 14; managerial view, 35; process, 95, 110, 113, 124, 140, 147

value creation, for stakeholders: assessing stakeholder strategies, 113, 116, *115;* behavior analysis, 109–111; changing the rules, 118–119; creating new modes of interaction, 122–130; developing integrative strategies, 116–117, *117;* holding strategies, 122; stakeholder assessment, 104, *105, 107,* 109; stakeholder interests, 10, 46, 48, 52–53, 54, *60,* 67, 84, *105,* 106, 126, 130, 160, 162; understanding stakeholders in more depth, 111–113

voluntarism, 42, 55, *60*

Wal-Mart, 12–13, 36, 37, 54, 76, 86, 89, 92, 153, 169; "everyday low price" as purpose at, 86

Werhane, Patricia H., 168, 169

Whole Foods Market: 95–96; "Conscious Capitalism," 167; Declaration of Interdependence, 95, 167; John Mackey (CEO), 167

Wilson, Sloan, 32

World Trade Organization (WTO), 29, 39

Wynbrandt, James, 168

Young, Andrew, 126–127

Yunus, Mohammed. *See* Grameen Bank